PRAISE FOR *SING!*

"The beauty of this book is how consistent it is with who and what the Gettys have been to the Church over the past decade. Their contribution is not significant because of the extraordinary but the ordinary. They are ordinary Christians who have made an extraordinary impact, not because of their musical or theological credentials, but because of their desire and willingness to devote themselves to the ordinary things. *Sing!* is an exposition of those ordinary things that have allowed the Gettys to be used by the Lord to bless, encourage, and provoke so many of us not only to 'sing to the Lord a new song,' but also to love and appreciate the old ones. May this practical, pastoral, theological, accessible, and delightful book help and bless many. May it encourage us all to *Sing!*"

Voddie Baucham Jr., dean of Theological Education, African Christian University in Lusaka, Zambia

"Here is a book worth buying. Filled with biblical, practical insight that, understood and taken to heart, will revolutionize congregational singing."

Alistair Begg, pastor of Truth for Life Radio and general editor of the *CSB Spurgeon Study Bible*

"*Sing!* is wonderful! It's a treasury of lost principles discovered for a new generation of worshippers. *Sing!* reminds me and my family that God uses music and the Word to transform the world, and that our part in His process of renewing all things is to open our mouths."

Kirk Cameron, film actor and producer

"With a rare combination of theological insight, the lessons shaped by years of practical experience, and remarkable readability, this book is simultaneously evocative, informative, and accessible."

D. A. Carson, author, president and founder of The Gospel Coalition

"The Gettys have been helping us sing for years now by the songs they've written. Now they help us in a different way. This book encourages us to realize that singing is an important part of spiritual life. Each chapter is short and readable. Each one also ends with good questions. Useful for individuals, Bible studies, or Sunday school classes—read, enjoy, discuss—and sing!"

Mark Dever, senior pastor of Capitol Hill
Baptist Church, Washington D.C.

"If there is an area in special need of reformation in the worship of evangelical churches, it is congregational singing. I am so thankful for the Gettys' hearts for this vital aspect of our communion with God. One place for us to begin this recovery is to understand why singing together is so important. This book will help. People and pastors alike need to read it."

Ligon Duncan, president of
Reformed Theological Seminary

"This practical book has four outstanding characteristics: it is written by seasoned musicians and song writers; it challenges the whole body of Christ, including pastoral and worship leaders, and professional Christian musicians, to worship meaningfully; it touches personal, family and congregational worship; and, it provides useful discussion questions that give a framework for group study and reflection. This book will be used widely to promote singing and worship in the church."

Matthew Ebenezer, teaching elder of
Reformed Presbyterian Church of India and author of
What the Apostles Believed: A Devotional Commentary

"Keith and Kristyn's music has always inspired my worship and deepened my faith at the same time. In an era when much contemporary Christian music is vapid, shallow, and theologically flimsy, they are a two-person reformation team whose songs will stand the test of time."

Os Guinness, author of *The Call*

"Somewhere along the way, it seems the Western church began to believe that singing was for singers. With this book, the Gettys have brought us back to the essential truth that singing is for believers. Once we understand that, the question, 'Do you have a voice?' changes to, 'Do you have a song?' *Sing!* helps us discover all the reasons God put a new song in our hearts the moment we met Him. Thank you, Keith and Kristyn, for this vital message."

Mike Harland, director of Worship,
Lifeway Christian Resources

"This book sparkles with ideas. In this bedeviled world there's no greater joy than profound truths of Jesus' love borne by great text and tune, and carried from Sunday into life and life eternal. That's what the Gettys do. Here's 'Why?' and 'How?'"

Matthew Harrison, president of LCMS

"Keith and Kristyn have served the church for years through their songs. Now they've gone one step further and served us with their book, *Sing!*. It's a treasure trove of biblical, practical, and gospel counsel for those who love to sing, want to sing, or don't think they can sing."

Bob Kauflin, director of Sovereign Grace Music

"This book reminds us that often the most effective means of catechizing our children will come as we teach them the great truths contained in the lyrics of the songs, hymns, and spiritual songs we sing together as a family. I'm hoping this book will motivate more moms and dads to make sure their children memorize the songs of Watts, Wesley, Toplady, and so many others."

Bob Lepine, vice president of
FamilyLife Today, radio host

"Jonathan Edwards said that 'no light in the understanding is good which does not produce holy affection in the heart.' Both in their music and now in this book, Keith and Kristyn Getty demonstrate how God-centered singing creates 'holy affection' in the hearts of God's people. I therefore urge any who are concerned to bring our

God the worship He deserves to read this book alongside Edwards' *Treatise on Religious Affections*."

Samuel Logan, president emeritus of Westminster Theological Seminary (PA) and associate international director of The World Reformed Fellowship

"I love Keith and Kristyn Getty! As friends. As songwriters. As worship leaders. They never fail to uplift and inspire my heart to sing! I pray that not only their music but this book will do the same for others."

Anne Graham Lotz, author, speaker, and daughter of Billy Graham

"The Gettys are a precious benediction from heaven to enrich our praise. They have been used by the Lord to provide theologically rich, singable music for the church in this generation. More than anyone else they have led in the long-awaited revival of hymns which have always been the true music of the church."

John MacArthur, pastor-teacher of Grace Community Church

"As I've monitored trends in today's church music, I've longed for someone with insight and courage to write a book like this. It's not enough to recommend it to you. I also recommend you pass it along to your church, your small group, your choir, and even the friends on your Christmas list. We need to talk about what's happening to today's worship. We need to make sure we're singing to the Lord with all His truth flowing through our hearts and filling our lungs and pleasing our Lord. We're made for this, but we're missing this. Let Keith and Kristyn give you voice lessons for the soul with this book that rings with their convictions and experiences. Read it and sing!"

Robert Morgan, author of *Then Sings My Soul*

"I have read a lot about worship and about music in worship— but never before just about singing! What a wonderful subject, and what a wonderful book. I did not think I needed yet another reason to be grateful to Keith and Kristyn Getty. But now I have one!"

Richard Mouw, president emeritus of
Fuller Theological Seminary

"One of Martin Luther's earliest books stressed two things essential to the church service: the sermon and congregational singing. This book by the Gettys makes an urgent call to Christians in our day not to forfeit our great privilege to sing the praise due to our Creator and Redeemer. Read it and, then, sing."

Stephen J. Nichols, president of Reformation
Bible College and chief academic officer,
Ligonier Ministries

"Keith and Kristyn Getty are good friends of mine and good gifts from God to His Church. They teach, help, and lead us to sing in a way that reveres the holiness of God, reflects the Word of God, edifies the Church of God, and compels us on mission for God in a world that desperately needs to know His glory."

David Platt, author of *Radical* and
president of the International Mission Board

"Keith and Kristyn have been an inspiration to me, as well as many others. This great book is a challenging treatise on Christian singing that every pastor and worship leader regardless of any culture, should put into practice along with the Bible in order that the church's singing becomes a major part of what the life-changing experience of worship is."

Yusin Pons, worship leader and songwriter,
Baptist Convention of Western Cuba

"*Sing!* is not just a book; it's a revolution. The music of Keith and Kristyn Getty has been a movement in our churches. Now this book will take the movement from the platform to the congregation.

What a gift the Gettys are to our churches. What a gift this book is for our churches' future."

"There are many who sing 'out of love for the art.' Although this sounds very artistic, when we talk about singing to God, doing so 'out of love for the art' is not enough. Keith and Kristyn combine biblical precision and agile writing to show us the privilege and beauty of worshipping our Lord through song. This very easy-to-read book has already become a reference that will certainly aid me in the formation of a new generation of worshippers, in the personal as well as in the family and congregational context."

"I'm more than excited by Keith and Kristyn's new book: it's short, highly readable, while making a profoundly compelling case for singing as a key discipling tool in our personal lives, our families, the church, and even in reaching the 'millennials.' I particularly like the 'bonus track' for pastors as a catalyst for making sure I am being faithful in encouraging my congregation to sing to God's glory. This book is a real gift to the twenty-first-century Church. It literally makes you want to sing!"

"I absolutely loved this book. Why? Because it had a great tone, was deep and rich, biblical, practical, informative, insightful, and helpful. Excuse the pun, but they are singing my tune. It should be required reading for all contemporary song writers (other than Keith and Kristyn, of course!)."

"We know and often gladly use the Gettys' music in our local church. In our opinion it meets the biblical criteria for church music. They are wonderful songs, on all levels, and make a deep impact in the lives of worshippers."

E. J. (Rassie) Smit, chairperson of
The Liturgical Commission of the General Synod
of the Reformed Churches, South Africa

"Congregational singing seems to be the biblical command that many have forgotten. Here in *Sing!* the Gettys tell us why it matters and how to bring it back. You and your church need this book."

Ed Stetzer, Billy Graham
distinguished chair, Wheaton College

"Few capture the vision of the true purpose of congregational worship like my friend Keith Getty. In the same way his songs have blessed us for decades, this book is a gift to the church and inspiring to anyone who longs to understand how near our corporate song is to the heart of God."

Laura Story, worship leader and songwriter
("Indescribable", "Blessings")

"It's one thing to sing a praise song to God by yourself; it's quite another when Christian friends join in with harmony. God designed and created us to sing together! Keith and Kristyn have a passion to get the church singing communally with voices blending in sweet accord, and their remarkable new book *Sing!* serves as a practical guide to reintroduce the church to classic and current hymns of the faith. You can help bring a fresh, Spirit-blessed ministry of music to your small group or congregation, just using the book you hold in your hands . . . so flip the page and get singing!"

Joni Eareckson Tada, Joni and Friends
International Disability Center

"I am thankful for the music of Keith and Kristyn Getty. Their music has been embraced globally, and Australian churches in particular have been encouraged to find their singing voice through their timeless hymns. I have seen diverse congregations around Australia, of every age group, find a common voice through Keith and Kristyn's excellent, singable, and deeply rich hymns. I couldn't be more thankful for this new book *Sing!* and look forward to Aussie churches finding yet another wonderful resource from the Gettys to encourage us to enjoy our singing and allow our singing to help shape our mission as a part of the global church.

"I've had the privilege of sitting in on many of Keith's training days as we have traveled around the United States, and now all of that insight and encouragement is in this new book *Sing!*. As someone who has seen younger generations in Australia engage with the beauty of the gospel through Keith and Kristyn's hymns, I am thankful for their passion to encourage the global church to sing, most obviously through their own timeless and excellent hymn writing, and now in their latest resource for churches everywhere, *Sing!*."

Nathan Tasker, award-winning Australian singer-songwriter, speaker, and director of Art House, Nashville, Tennessee

"As someone who seeks to communicate the Word of God I'm so aware that songs have great power to teach. They reach into the heart and mobilize the will in such a profound way, and I'm therefore deeply grateful for the faithfulness to Scripture that characterizes Keith and Kristyn's hymns. Songs bring us to the truth or cause us to sway from the truth and, therefore, we must celebrate those whose musical gifts are so wonderfully under the authority of Scripture."

Rico Tice, senior minister, All Souls Langham Place, founder, Christianity Explored Ministries, and author of *Honest Evangelism* and *Capturing God*

"In *Sing!* Keith and Kristyn describe some of the essential themes that have shaped and renewed our congregational singing here at

The Village Chapel. *Sing!* informs, inspires, and encourages church leaders to consider how they can lead their congregations to a more robust worship of the living God. An essential read, an essential call, at an essential time.

Jim Thomas, pastor of The Village Chapel,
Nashville, Tennessee

"I know of no book that does what the Gettys' book on congregational singing does. It is informative, convicting, and motivating and every pastor and serious Christian should read it."

Paul Tripp, author and president of Paul Tripp Ministries

"One of the church's greatest treasures is congregational singing. When you join your voice to those of your brothers and sisters in praise of King Jesus, you are looking up to God as Redeemer and around to the people who have been redeemed. *Sing!* is a book of encouragement, warning, and guidance that will help ensure that the next generation does not lose the precious treasure of singing together."

Trevin Wax, author of *This Is Our Time*,
Counterfeit Gospels, and *Gospel-Centered Teaching*

"As a follower of Jesus, husband, father, grandfather, and pastor, *Sing!* hits a sphere of our life that is not addressed enough: singing and our spiritual formation as people and especially in community. As a pastor, the latter is particularly meaningful (and helpful) to me."

Dean Weaver, lead pastor of Memorial Park
and moderator of Evangelical Presbyterian Church

"Keith and Kristyn Getty have given their lives to demonstrate the power of doctrinally-faithful hymns old and new, inspiring a new generation of hymn-lovers. Now they have written a wonderful book to show us why and how this can be done. We enthusiastically commend it to you."

Robert and Nancy (DeMoss) Wolgemuth, authors/speakers
who love to sing to the Lord

Sing!

How Worship Transforms
Your Life, Family, and Church

KEITH and KRISTYN GETTY

B&H
PUBLISHING GROUP

NASHVILLE, TENNESSEE

978-1-4627-4266-0

Published by B&H Publishing Group
Nashville, Tennessee

Dewey Decimal Classification: 264.2
Subject Heading: WORSHIP \ PUBLIC WORSHIP \ SINGING

4 5 6 7 8 9 10 • 22 21 20 19 18

*Dedicated to the three little singers
the Lord has given us—
our daughters, Eliza, Charlotte, and Grace.*

CONTENTS

How to Use This Book   xvii

Prelude: Sing!   xix

Chapter 1. Created to . . . Sing!   1

Chapter 2. Commanded to . . . Sing!   13

Chapter 3. Compelled to . . . Sing!   21

Chapter 4. Sing! . . . with Heart and Mind   37

Chapter 5. Sing! . . . with Your Family   53

Chapter 6. Sing! . . . with the Local Church   71

Chapter 7. The Radical Witness When Congregations . . . Sing! 85

Postlude: Will You Sing?   97

Bonus Tracks   103

   •   Track One: For Pastors and Elders   105

   •   Track Two: Worship and Song Leaders   113

   •   Track Three: Musicians, Choirs, and Production   123

   •   Track Four: Songwriters and Creatives   133

Acknowledgments   143

Notes   147

HOW TO USE THIS BOOK

This book is intended to be a straightforward and helpful read to individuals, but we have organized the book in such a way that it might inspire group discussion within whole churches. As it deals with a theme that depends on community, the ideal reading of this book is within a community of readers, or rather a community of singers (which we all are). To that end, here are a few thoughts on its use:

I. A 6-Week Churchwide Campaign

To help galvanize all church members in the call to be a singing church, culminating in an evening churchwide or citywide hymn sing

II. In a Book Club or Group

Multiple groups at a church, or perhaps just those that gather on a special night of the week

III. Among Leaders and Among Choirs and Music Groups

Pastors, staff, and lay leaders (at the end of this book, you will find "Bonus Tracks," that are additional content geared toward leaders)

SING!

Come, let us sing for joy to the LORD, let us
shout aloud to the Rock of our salvation. Let us
come before him with thanksgiving and extol
him with music and song. (Ps. 95:1–2)

We need to talk about singing.

Singing is why, in 2006, we moved from the most beautiful lit-tle emerald isle on Earth to a new and wonderful home in America. We came over from Northern Ireland to tour and to steward our hymn-writing, both throughout the US and worldwide. While most of our work has been musical—singing and playing—over the years we have gradually found ourselves talking more and more about singing. Not about up-front singing, but whole-church sing-ing—congregational singing. That's a kind of singing that we never tire of talking about—not just because as Irish people we like to talk, but because as Christians we think this is something about which we *need* to talk.

Early on in our time touring, we began to hold leadership lunches as part of our stay in a particular city. These were basically conversations over food about church music, for pastors and music leaders in that city. Over time, we noticed the attendees would ask thoughtful questions about song style, song choice, songwriting, production, relationships, training, sound, and so on—but there was one question we were rarely, if ever, hearing as they reflected on their own churches:

"How did the congregation sing?"

The congregation's singing did not appear to be a key factor, let alone the primary one, in determining how well the music in a worship service had gone. Hardly anyone asked us to talk about it.

Maybe you don't much want to talk about it either.

Perhaps for you, singing is always a painful part of church life, because someone who once stood beside you is not there anymore, or because your struggles in the week seem to tighten your vocal chords on a Sunday.

Perhaps you simply don't have much time to think about it, because you are a parent tumbling in fresh from the battle of trying to get the whole family out to church; under-slept, overly caffeinated, and singing with one eye on the screen and one on your children, longing for these sung truths to be the air blowing through their souls (we know this feeling very well).

Perhaps, though, you are starting to think about it because you're a student, and the increasing complexities of life and study and faith don't always seem to connect with what you sing on a Sunday.

Or perhaps you long to talk confidently about it, because you are a leader or pastor yearning for people to sing to their core the things you are teaching, but you're not sure how to navigate the maze of church music, or where you want your church's music to get to anyway.

Yet whatever you think about singing, the truth is that we are all invited into the same musical home. For the Church has been, is, and always should be and can be a joyfully singing Church. In a sense, singing is part of what we exist to do. The apostle Peter wrote to local churches that each of them was part of "a chosen people, a royal priesthood, a holy nation, God's special possession, that you may declare the excellencies of him who called you out of darkness into his wonderful light" (1 Pet. 2:9 ESV). Paul told the members of the church in Ephesus to be "speaking to one another with psalms, hymns, and songs from the Spirit." He wanted them to "sing and make music from your heart to the Lord, always giving thanks to God the Father for everything, in the name of our Lord Jesus Christ" (Eph. 5:19–20).

Though maybe misunderstood, regularly a bone of contention, and often under-practiced, congregational singing is one of the greatest and most beautiful tools we have been given to declare

God's "excellencies," strengthening His Church and sharing His glory with the world.

The New Testament implies that our singing is important. It's been said that Christians are a singing people—but often, many of us are really more of a mouthing-along-with-the-words kind of people.

This book is about singing together as the church in a way that impacts all of your life. It is a conversation for the whole church, including you, whether your singing voice is a close friend to you or more of an awkward stranger. It explores something that is part of the worship life of every follower of Christ. There are many books helping us to grow and train in our Bible study and prayer and acts of service and evangelism, but not very many helping us to sing. Yet our singing deserves similar care, and is even (as we'll see) tied to the flourishing of these other things in our lives.

How did the congregation sing? Each of us is part of the answer to that in our own church, whether we are on stage or standing by our seat on the main floor. It's a harder and in some ways less comfortable question than all the other ones people tend to ask about the music in church. Yet Paul does not tell us to perform for one another, but to sing to one another. We need to ask, "How did the congregation sing?"

LUTHER THE SINGER

Five hundred years ago, in the autumn of 1517, a German monk named Martin Luther began what became known as the "reformation" of the church through the preaching and the singing of the Word. You might understandably think of Luther primarily as a theologian, or preacher, but he was also a focused and prolific hymn-writer, who reinvigorated singing in what became known as the Protestant church. How the congregation sang was a key question for Luther; he believed that a truly biblical church would be one where every believer was actively participating in every part of the service, including the singing, celebrating this incredible gospel together:

> Let God speak directly to His people through the Scriptures, and let His people respond with grateful songs of praise.[1]

Many of Luther's enemies feared his hymns more than the man himself. Singing was at the heart of the Reformation—indeed, such was the conviction of the man who was in some ways Luther's predecessor, the Bohemian Jan Huss, that he was martyred for (among other things) speaking the "heresy of congregational singing."

Luther was passionate and serious about the art and practice of music and congregational singing—a passion that today in many churches has arguably lost its focus. The theologian Ligon Duncan has said, "There is no part of the worship life more in need of reformation today than congregational singing." But this reformation will not come by simply telling people to sing, any more than telling a child to eat something they don't like makes much difference for very long. We need not only to know that we ought to sing as Christians, but to learn to love to sing as Christians.

THE FIVE GOALS OF THIS BOOK

This book has been years in the making (partly due to a promise we made to a good friend that we wouldn't write a book until Keith passed his fortieth birthday). Grown from our passion for congregational singing, it's been formed in our traveling and playing and listening and discussing and learning and teaching. And in writing it, we have five key aims:

1. To discover why we sing and the overwhelming joy and holy privilege that comes with singing
2. To consider how singing impacts our hearts and minds and all of our lives
3. To cultivate a culture of family singing in our daily home life
4. To equip our churches for wholeheartedly singing to the Lord and one another as an expression of unity
5. To inspire us to see congregational singing as a radical witness to the world

We have also added a few "bonus tracks" at the end with some more practical suggestions for different groups who are more deeply involved with church singing.

But just before we start, a health warning.

We want to be practical—but not prescriptive. We realize (and it is worth you realizing) that we are all limited by our own experiences. It is easy to assume that what we are used to or what we most enjoy is what God is most pleased by. Of course there are principles that transcend styles, but we naturally bring our own personality and bias to such an emotional subject as Christian singing. Yet in congregational singing, there is no one-style-fits-all template. We love singing at our home church in our community in Nashville. The Village Chapel uses acoustic musicians almost hidden in the corner of the room to accompany beautiful singing of three to four hundred on a Sunday, which often drops to a capella in rich harmony. And we also love to lead singing at Times Square Church in New York City, which has a diverse congregation from more than one hundred countries, a vibrant Pentecostal gospel choir, and high-energy music. We have sung praise with thousands, and with just a few; we have played with full orchestras, and without any musical accompaniment at all. And each has been engaging, sincere praise that is authentic to that particular community and tradition. The more we interact with churches around the world, the more we are amazed at the beauty and colors and splendor of God's creativity reflected in people singing His praise.

And God intends for that people—a people joyfully joining together in song with brothers and sisters around the world and around His heavenly throne—to include you. He wants you, He wants us, to sing.

DISCUSSION QUESTIONS

1. How has singing played a role in your spiritual development?

2. Can you recall an example of a memorable occasion where you enjoyed singing in church? What about that event made an impact on you?

3. Are you quick to assess the music in your church by style, performance, and stage, or by the quality of the congregation's singing?

4. What is your desire for the singing in your church?

CHAPTER 1

CREATED TO . . . SING!

We are a singing people because it is how God has created us. It's what we do.

And when we do, we're simply joining in with what the rest of creation is doing.

DESIGNED TO SING

We are all singers. We may not all be very good singers, but we are all created to be singers nonetheless.

The psalmist sings, "For you created my inmost being; you knit me together in my mother's womb. I praise you because I am fearfully and wonderfully made" (Ps. 139:13–14). We have three young daughters, and it has surprised us with each of them how early they could sing. Simple melodies with mumbled words grew into phrases like "O sing happylujah," or a bizarre mixture of "Holy,

Holy, Holy, Lord God Almighty" and "Twinkle, Twinkle Little Star."
To sing is written into our human DNA; it is part of God's design.
Our desire to make musical instruments to accompany our singing
is as old as our desire to fashion tools to aid us in our daily work
(Gen. 4:21–22). Throughout Scripture and through history, we see
God's people using this gift of song to praise Him, the Giver of it.

Your ability to sing is fearfully and wonderfully made. Around
the twelve-week mark, the vocal cords of a baby growing in the
womb are in place and have been shown to work long before the
baby is born. We may sound different, but each of us has the same
vocal apparatus (you, us, Bono, Pavarotti, Sinatra)—breath flowing
up from our lungs, vibrating through vocal cords in our throat, and
pushing sound out through the articulators of our mouths, tongues,
and lips. Singing is not merely a happy by-product of God's real
intent of making us creatures who can speak. It is something we're
designed to be able to do.

But not only that, God designed our psyche for singing. When
singing praise to God, so much more than just the vocal box is
engaged. God has created our minds to judge pitch and lyric; to
think through the concepts we sing; to engage the intellect, imagination, and memory; and to remember what is set to a tune (we
are confident that, right now, 99 percent of this book's readers can
remember more lyrics set to music than can recite Scripture by
rote). God has formed our hearts to be moved with depth of feeling
and a whole range of emotion as the melody-carried truths of who
God is and whose we are sink in.

WHAT IF I "CAN'T SING"?

Sometimes we meet people who say, "I can't sing"—as in, "The sound that comes out of my mouth when I try to sing is not what I was hoping for."

Perhaps this is you, and you can recall an awkward conversation as a child when you were asked to mouth the words, rather than sing them; or when it was suggested that being a member of your school or church choir might not be the best fit for your gifts.

But if you can speak, you can physically sing. The truth is that God designed you to sing and gave you everything you need to sing, as well as He wants you to. He's far less concerned with your tunefulness than your integrity. Christian singing begins with the heart, not on the lips (Eph. 5:19).

Because they are very little and are at different stages of learning to sing, when our daughters sing together, the older is more confident than the middle one, who is in turn more fluent than the youngest. This may change as they all get older, but the point is this—to their parents' ears, each voice is not only as important as the others but is as treasured as the others. Your heavenly Father cares whether and what you sing, but He does not mind how well you sing. While we may have choirs within our churches made up of voices who have expertise and ability, the congregation of a church is the ultimate choir, and it is without auditions—everyone can be in it and should be in it.

The true beauty of such a congregational choir is that our voices and our hearts are knit *together* in praise. It is exhilarating to be part of a body of believers singing truth *together*. We recently met with a missionary to China who was home on furlough in America. After the singing, he said how wonderful it was to be able to sing freely with other believers again, for the part of China he lived in imposed heavy restrictions on such a thing. "Oh, how my heart misses the singing," he said. Your voice may not be of professional standard, but it is of confessional standard.

It is worth adding, though, that the more we practice something, the better we become at it—and we seek to improve in what we truly value. "As with almost everything worthwhile in life, there is rarely just one day to do it."[2] To learn to walk takes time, and we first must learn to press down on our feet. To learn to speak takes time, and we must first open our mouths and make sounds. To praise God in tuneful song takes time, and we grow better at singing by singing. And once we've reached our peak, if it is still some way short of the tuneful heights, a sense of humor is a useful ally. Some people do have a special gift of singing absolutely every note slightly off pitch (which is, ironically, very hard to do). Since we sing to encourage and praise, not to impress and earn praise, we can smile about that and sing anyway.

One of our band members, Zach White, recently told us of the inspiration his dad has been to him and his siblings when it comes to singing in church. Mr. White is always the most passionate singer in the congregation, despite only having three notes he can actually sing (all lower than his namesake, Barry), and none of them in tune. But it never holds him back. He has grasped what congregational singing is, and is not, about.

Kristyn's vocal coach for the last fourteen years, Kim Wood Sandusky, has several decades of experience in training professional singers across genres. She points out that "we are all singers. Some of us have talents that allow us to sing with beautiful tones and good pitch, while others have talents to sing with their soul. What a beautiful sound we all make as singers to our heavenly Father's ears."

There are those of us who may have vocal constrictions that come through health struggles or have been there since birth. If you cannot speak but sing by signing with your hands or through whatever means God has given you, you bless the community of believers as we join with one heart and one voice until the day all tongues will sing to Him. We are so grateful for the work of signers who enable the whole congregation to so meaningfully engage in the lyrics we sing.

SINGING IN HIS IMAGE

Since God is a creator who enjoys beauty, it follows that we, as those creatures uniquely made in His image (Gen. 1:26–28), will do so too. What God made has beauty as well as functionality: "The LORD God made all kinds of trees grow out of the ground—trees that were pleasing to the eye *and* good for food" (Gen. 2:9, our italics).

We have been created to *enjoy* beauty and enjoy creativity. You don't have to go to an art museum to understand this—but simply as far as the special occasion dinner date with your spouse, where you don't want the food just to be passable but irresistible to the eyes and the palate; and you don't just want a roof to keep the rain out, but a beautiful and meaningful place to make a memory of it. We can tell the difference between an orchestra tuning up and them then playing a coherent piece of music—suddenly, there is a "rightness" in how the notes sit together. We know that sense of throwing back your head or raising your hands to sing a great hymn with every ounce of your being and the feeling of losing interest in a mediocre one. This is why for a songwriter, it's worth striving day after day for months (or years) to compose that one melodic idea that is fresh, compelling, and might touch another person's soul.

We are designed to benefit from beauty in creativity. Have you ever wondered why we sing our national anthems and don't just recite their lyrics, or why as children we learn our alphabet in rhyming songs rather than simply as a series of monotone spoken sounds? It's because God made us to be powerfully engaged in our senses and memories by music. Songs have the power to prompt a memory or transport us back to some other time and place. Our sense of imagination is another aspect of the dignity we have been given as human beings by God. It should not be belittled but embraced and nurtured, especially by the artistic endeavors of every local church. They reach the inner corridors of our soul in a way that other things cannot. This is part of why we tend to have such heated conversations about what we like in church music—because it moves us so deeply. We are designed as beauty-appreciators. It matters to us.

We have also been made to like making things ourselves. J. R. R. Tolkien wrote that "we are not only made, but made in the image and likeness of a Maker."[3] We show our God-inspired creative spirit when we make music—not just in the songs themselves, but in the many different creative ways we arrange and express the songs together. Whether it is the rhythmic vibrancy of sung worship led by the African Children's Choir, or the pristine beauty of a chorale echoing within the ancient walls of a European cathedral, or the blended accents in the increasing number of international churches in cities around the world, we seek to create beauty because that's how we're designed.

And as we create, we communicate—just as God does through His creation:

> The heavens declare the glory of God;
>> the skies proclaim the work of his hands.
> Day after day they pour forth speech;
>> night after night they reveal knowledge.
> (Ps. 19:1–2)

Echoing through our congregational singing is the communication the divine Author has written into this world. Melodies matter. Words matter. Our songs always say something. We have been created to use language, to reflect and meditate on His words, to remember over and over again His voice. Singing together organizes notes and words in beautiful ways to shine God's dazzling truths into the relativistic grays of our culture.

Equally wonderfully, we are designed not only to be able to create songs about God but to God. It is an incredible thing that we, the created ones, have been given a way to communicate with the One who made us. We sing knowing that our Lord's ears are open and listening as we lift our voices to Him with intelligent, sincere, and joy-filled words and notes. Our singing is not like prayer—it *is* prayer. And the great sixth-century church father St. Augustine is reputed to have said that we pray twice when we sing.

As we sing to God and about God together with the people of God, we reflect the truth that we were designed for community, both with God and with each other. It was never good for man to be alone, and singing together engenders and expresses that we are family. When we sing, we show the community that reflects our Creator, our triune God. When His Church sings together, voice upon voice like arms linked across a room, and indeed across all the gathering places of His followers around the globe, across history, we are doing what we were designed to enjoy—using our God-given voices to sing praises together to the One who gave us those voices. It expresses what unites us, and it reminds us of our interdependence.

SINGING WITH CREATION

Creation sings the Father's song. When we sing as God's people, it brings us into line with the whole of the rest of creation:

> Shout for joy to the LORD, all the earth,
>> burst into jubilant song with music;
> make music to the LORD with the harp,
>> with the harp and the sound of singing,
> with trumpets and the blast of the ram's horn—
>> shout for joy before the LORD, the King.
> Let the sea resound, and everything in it,
>> the world, and all who live in it.
> Let the rivers clap their hands,
>> let the mountains sing together for joy;
> let them sing before the LORD,
>> for he comes to judge the earth.
> He will judge the world in righteousness
>> and the peoples with equity. (Ps. 98:4–9)

"What is the chief end of man?" asks the Westminster Shorter Catechism. The answer: "To glorify God and enjoy Him forever." To praise Him is the original desire sewn into every fiber of our God-designed humanity and into every aspect of our God-designed world. When we sing God's praise, we join with the tune of the cosmos. Just pause. Isn't this incredible?

In C. S. Lewis's *The Magician's Nephew*, the great lion Aslan creates Narnia by singing it into existence. The character and timbre of the song are seen in the shapes and colors of all that springs up out of the nothingness. Lewis delights to point out that the song could not be separated from the Singer and that when your eyes saw the Singer He eclipsed everything else.

We are created to sing because it leads us joyfully to the great Singer, Creator of the heavens and the earth. Paul Tripp writes, "God is the ultimate musician. His music transforms your life. The notes of redemption rearrange your heart and restore your life. His songs of forgiveness, grace, reconciliation, truth, hope, sovereignty, and love give you back your humanity and restore your identity."[4]

Our singing should sound like Him, look like Him, and lead our hearts to Him. When the psalmist sings, "I lift my eyes up to the hills, where does my help come from?" (Ps. 121 NIV 1984), his help does not come from those hills, but from He who made the hills. We do not worship the created art of singing; we worship Him. Don't sing primarily because you love singing, or keep quiet because you do not. Sing because you love who made you, and formed you, and enables you to sing:

> *We sing to Him, whose wisdom form'd the ear,*
> *our songs, let Him who gave us voices, hear;*
> *we joy in God, who is the Spring of mirth,*
> *who loves the harmony of Heav'n and Earth;*

our humble sonnets shall that praise rehearse,
who is the music of the Universe.
And whilst we sing, we consecrate our art,
and offer up with ev'ry tongue a heart.
(Nathaniel Ingelo, 1688)

DISCUSSION QUESTIONS

1. Can you recall your earliest memory of singing? How did it make you feel?

2. What do you experience during congregational singing—feelings like joy, fear, self-consciousness, freedom, etc.?

3. What kind of "practice" might your church do to help members feel more confident, less self-aware, and more engaged in hymn singing?

CHAPTER 2

COMMANDED TO . . . SING!

We are a singing people because God has commanded us to sing.

It's what we do.

Kristyn remembers being in the kitchen with her mum as a teenager having a conversation with her about prayer. Growing up in a Christian home, she had been taught about, shown, and helped with praying. But on this day, she was dragging her feet over the idea of praying and was somewhat overcomplicating the process (something that, in future years, her husband would not find hard to believe!). After a little while, her mum, with her kind, strong eyes, very simply said, "At the end of the day, we are commanded by God to pray—so we must do it!"

The same is equally true of singing. We are commanded by God to sing—so we must do it. Not to sing is to disobey.

God's commands are not arbitrary—they are always for His people's good. Part of the glory of God's commands are that His law is the "perfect law that gives freedom" (James 1:25). Just as we are told to study the Scriptures, to pray, to give, to take communion, so we are commanded to sing with the saints because we need to sing. Our spiritual health depends on it.

It is of course not a clinical obedience, without warmth of conviction or joy of relationship (which we will talk about in the next chapter). But it is a matter of obedience. As the great hymn-writer John Newton once wrote,

> *Our pleasure and our duty,*
> *Though opposite before;*
> *Since we have seen his beauty,*
> *Are joined to part no more.*[5]

Christian singing is far more than doing our duty, but it is never less. We are *commanded* to, "Sing to the LORD a new song, his praise in the assembly of the saints" (Ps. 149:1).

Repeatedly and throughout Scripture, we are commanded to be a singing people. There are more than four hundred references to singing in the Bible and at least fifty direct commands. We are not to disregard the command because we don't like the music or the personnel or are not in the mood. The command in Psalm 149:1 contains no caveats or conditions. It should go without saying that the leadership of a church should be facilitating congregational singing so that we can all honor the Lord in this together. We are told to sing—and the Scripture is not only concerned *that* we sing but also with where, what, and how we sing.

WHERE WE SING

The command is not to sing just into ourselves or by ourselves (like in the shower or in the car), but out loud as part of "the assembly of the saints"—that is, in the company of other believers, with your church. It is not a metaphorical or optional or seasonal suggestion, but a clear directive from our Lord and Savior to sing as a regular part of our worship life, primarily and especially with other believers. We are not to think of it as "just the singing"—something we can skip over or arrive late for—but something we are to take seriously, to value, to set aside time for.

It may sound like a rather obvious statement to make, but in the assembly each of us will not be in the majority. That means you are going to be singing songs you may not have chosen because they are not your favorite, to arrangements or with accompaniment that you may not have chosen because they are not your favorites. You are going to need to be willing to lay down your own tastes for the good of the wider assembly. For as long as we have the health and the ability, we are each called to sing with the people of God, and to love our people enough to serve each other in the way we sing.

WHAT WE SING

We have so much creative freedom in our music and songs, which of course is magnificently seen in the diversity of sounds and styles expressed in the Church all over the world. But the Bible is more specific about *what* we should sing. In his letter to the Colossian church, Paul writes:

> Let the word of Christ dwell in you richly, teaching and admonishing one another in all wisdom, singing psalms and hymns and spiritual songs, with thankfulness in your hearts to God. (Col. 3:16 ESV)

One of the ways the Word of Jesus can dwell in us richly is for us to sing it to one another. We are commanded to sing the Word of God—the truth revealed in the Scriptures, the story of redemption. Fundamentally, we're to sing about God, revealed in Christ and supremely in His suffering and His glory, since that's what the Word of God is all about (Luke 24:26–27). "Richly" brings to mind words like *generously, magnificently, fully, thoroughly*. Content matters.

Tragically, many of the songs that are written for and sung in churches do not fulfill this description. If we only have space to sing a few songs on a Sunday, we need to make the time really count—to sing the best songs we can find. Why would we want to do anything less? We should be picky. The songs we sing should not brush along the surface, or pluck phrases out of context, or focus exclusively on ourselves, or describe Jesus in a way His Word does not (or, still worse, to speak in contradiction to His Word).

Every part of a lyric should link together to bring a wonderful, thoughtful, deep expression of Scripture to every singer. If you are choosing the songs as a worship leader, this is your responsibility (and we'll think more about that later). If you are singing the songs as a member of the assembly of the saints, then don't just sing, but think. What are you singing? How does it point you to Jesus as He reveals Himself in His Word? What truths are being laid on your heart, and how is your singing being used to lay them on the hearts of those around you? Which lines in the lyrics flood you with joy because they move you to consider Christ afresh, and how will you sing them to others and back to yourself this week? (More on this in chapter 5.)

We often ask people, "What do you think we should write a song about?" Years ago we led the music at a retreat for the Christian relief organization Medair in Switzerland. When we posed that question to the families who had gathered there from all over the world, we left with pages of topics and Bible verses we hadn't yet really thought of, that spoke into the intersection of the Christian faith and the physical and spiritual needs of the world. There is so much of the Word of Christ to sing! They wanted, and we should want, to sing deep things that affect all of life.

HOW WE SING

Colossians 3:16 also speaks into *how* we sing. The disposition of our hearts is not begrudging—"I sing because I must"—but rather "with thankfulness in your hearts to God"—"I sing because He is marvelous." Thankfulness is more than saying the words with your lips. In fact, you are not singing Christianly if you are singing only with your lips. The root of true thankfulness is the gratitude in our *hearts* for the unmerited benefits of God's goodness in our lives. This root blossoms into a good, positive, and loving attitude toward the call to sing from God and from the leaders He has given us in our churches.

It is hard—impossible, in fact—to sing what you are excited about in your spirit and grateful for in your heart in a way that is tepid, tentative, and withdrawn. Deeply felt thankfulness produces a sound from our voices that is robust and enthusiastic. What is happening when we sing is about so much more than the audible sound we create, but not less. How we sing does reveal how we think and feel about something. Most of us will all sing with some grit in a sports stadium or in a "happy birthday" at a loved one's party. Our individual personalities join up to make a collective personality, and our individual grateful hearts come together as the church. So as we obey the command to sing, we are (or should be) unleashing a congregational sound of conviction—whether there are a dozen of us or thousands of us. If we aren't, our children or visitors looking on have every right to wonder if what we are singing is truly important to us. In this sense, our singing betrays the truth about us, for better and for worse.

OUR SINGING SAVIOR

Jesus is, of course, supremely our salvation—but He is also our example. And our Lord Himself obeyed the command to sing. One of our favorite verses comes just after the retelling of the Lord's last supper on the night before He died for us, in Matthew 26. After Jesus told them to drink of the cup as a sign of His blood poured out for the forgiveness of sins, Matthew adds, "When they had sung a hymn, they went out to the Mount of Olives" (v. 30).

As He walked toward His arrest, Jesus *sang*. In the depths and heights of His passion, Jesus *sang*. Imagining the Lord Jesus singing with His followers a few short hours before the agony of the cross is an incredible and humbling thought. Even as He approached the darkest hour, our Savior was singing and leading these men in singing. Even on the cross itself, He famously quoted from a song, a psalm, that He would have grown up knowing. The songs He was trained in as a child sustained Him and, we might say, shaped Him through His most anguished moment of suffering;

> My God, my God why have you forsaken me? . . .
> My God, I cry out by day, but you do not answer,
> 　by night, but I find no rest.
> Yet you are enthroned as the Holy One;
> 　you are the one Israel praises. (Ps. 22:1–3)

How could we ever think we can be passive about singing?

As we digest the Word set in song and respond with thankfulness in our hearts to God, we are guided into His path of peace. That peace is Him. Singing, as with all these outward expressions of our worship, will never save us. But singing will help lead us to the One who will. The command to sing leads us to Christ with joy to praise and follow Him. How kind of God to command us to do something so wonderful!

DISCUSSION QUESTIONS

1. What response do you have personally to the "command to sing" praise to God?

2. How do you feel about singing not only songs you *like* but songs you *need* to sing?

3. What is the link between thankfulness and singing?

4. What are some things that might help you cultivate singing with intentional thankfulness?

CHAPTER 3

COMPELLED TO . . . SING!

We are a singing people because the gospel of the Lord Jesus *compels* us to sing. It's what we do.

Our good friend pastor Alistair Begg has spoken of how he can tell when someone who was on the sidelines of faith has embraced it by seeing them now with full eyes and fully engaged in the singing. Saved people are singing people.

Bob Kauflin writes in his book *Worship Matters* that,

Worship isn't primarily about music, techniques, songs or methodologies. It's about our hearts. It's about what and who we love more than anything.[6]

God's love for us inspires our response of love for Him and calls forth songs of joy from our lips.

We are compelled to sing. *Compelled*. What a strong and convicting word that is! Paul used it when defending his reasons for being so passionate about presenting an unblemished gospel to the church in Corinth. "For Christ's love compels us," he wrote, "because we are convinced that one died for all, and therefore all died. And he died for all, that those who live should no longer live for themselves but for him who died for them and was raised again" (2 Cor. 5:14–15).

Our motivation to sing comes from so much more than our-selves—our likes, our comfort levels, our musical tastes and prefer-ences. Intrinsically, it's driven by the One who died and was raised. It is driven by a heartfelt desire to convey gospel truth to those of us who already know it and need to be refreshed and renewed by it—and to communicate it to those who don't yet know, but who might be drawn to Christ through seeing and hearing people who clearly mean it because of the way that they sing about it.

CRIES OF FREEDOM

We are not compelled to sing out of thin air. Something—or rather, someone—stirs us to. When we were first learning to lead people in singing in our early twenties we heard something very helpful to us: Worship comes as a response to revelation.

We don't have to be in a church building to understand we are wired this way. When Ireland beats England in rugby (always a beautiful occasion), Keith and his dad cheer till they're hoarse. When we stand on the precipice of the Grand Canyon or at the jazz festival of Montreux at the foot of the French Alps, our eyes and hearts feast upon it. When we hear that a couple whom we love has become engaged, we exclaim our joy out loud. Praise is prompted by—compelled by—the revelation of something glorious.

And the gospel is the revelation of the most glorious truth in history. One of the songs we used to sing and play together when we first met was the spiritual "His Eye Is on the Sparrow," and there is a particular line we love: "I sing because I'm happy, I sing because I'm free." Such a simple but oh so profound a thought. We sing because we are *free*.

Jesus came so that we might know Him, the truth, for "the truth will set you free" (John 8:32). We were slaves to sin—while we chose to sin, sin was also our master. But God's Son died for our sins and rose to give us new life—"if the Son sets you free, you will be free indeed" (John 8:36). The gospel declares that "while we were still sinners, Christ died for us" (Rom. 5:8) so that now we know that "since we have now been justified by his blood, how much more shall we be saved from God's wrath through him" (v. 9). The gospel is a declaration of eternal freedom. It is a revelation that compels us to respond, and part of our response will be to sing.

We both became Christians as little children, so we don't remember that initial wave of freedom that rushes over someone who becomes a Christian later in life. But it doesn't take very long living as a Christian to know that sense of shame and frustration over sin—and then to remember,

When Satan tempts me to despair
And tells me of the guilt within
Upward I look and see Him there
Who made an end of all my sin,
Because the sinless Savior died,
My sinful soul is counted free,
For God the just is satisfied
To look on Him and pardon me.

(Charitie L. Bancroft, "Before the Throne of God Above," 1863)

Christ has broken every chain of sin that was tied around you, that you couldn't even see until He opened your eyes to see them. The chains of pride and selfishness, of broken desires and broken relationships—all shattered by His death. And you were not just freed *from* something, you were freed *for* something—to glorify Him, to live the life God designed you to live, to know life in all its forever fullness.

I sing because I'm free to run from all that tore me apart and to run to all that makes me whole. "The Spirit you received does not make you slaves, so that you live in fear again; rather, the Spirit you received brought about your adoption to sonship. And by him we cry, 'Abba, Father'" (Rom. 8:15). If I know this is true of me, in my heart as well as my head . . . well, it opens my mouth.

The truth is that we praise what we love. C. S. Lewis wrote, "I think we delight to praise what we enjoy because the praise not merely expresses but completes the enjoyment; it is its appointed consummation."[7]

In marriage, in family, and in friendship, we quickly discover that the joy of something is only half full until we've been able to tell someone else about it. Social media is filled with products, recipes, experiences, and ideas that we feel compelled to share with others. When our daughters paint pictures they're pleased with, they don't hide them in a drawer; they go up on the fridge for all to see and admire. It goes against the grain of how God created our humanity for us to keep from praising all that is praiseworthy, to keep quiet about what we are pleased with. Since God is most worthy of our praise, above all other things—since He is most deserving of our love, above all other people—we will respond not only by knowing we should praise Him, but by feeling we cannot help but praise Him, for it is our joy to do so, as well as our duty. And singing is one of the greatest ways we have to "complete the enjoyment" of all that the Lord has done for us and even more for who He is. As the beloved Irish missionary Amy Carmichael (1867–1951) wrote in her poem "A Song of Lovely Things":

> He put a new song in my mouth;
> His love is ever bringing/
> Cool leaves of healing from His tree;
> and though in drought
> How can I keep from singing?[8]

SCRIPTURE'S SALVATION SONGS

Throughout the unfolding story of Scripture, we can see this revelation-response prompt to sing praise. Let's consider five of these inspiring examples that help stir our hearts to the importance and outright joy of singing together.

1. The First Song

The first stated song recorded in Scripture is found in Exodus 15. It is a song of praise and thanksgiving sung by Moses and the Israelites on the eastern shore of the Red Sea after the Lord had brought them safely out of Egypt. They were celebrating a rescue and a victory: "The LORD is my strength and my song; he has become my salvation" (v. 2). Moses and Miriam helped teach and lead the Israelites, calling them to sing. Mirrored in this story is the gospel story of our rescue through Christ—and so we follow the lead of Moses and Miriam as we make Him and His death and resurrection the central theme of our singing. We stand on our own eastern shore, with our enemy defeated and death destroyed. We have been saved. And so we sing.

2. The Songs of Battle

Generations later, Deborah and the commander of Israel's fighting men, Barak, delivered a song to commemorate a stunning military reversal that freed God's people from twenty years of oppression to a Canaanite warlord (the event is recorded in Judges 4—the song of celebration in Judges 5). Singing turned the aftermath into a community event. Singing completed the joy of the victory.

The people sang when the ark of the covenant, having been recovered from the Philistines, was finally brought back to Jerusalem where David had prepared a special place for it (1 Chron. 15). They sang at the head of the armies, "Give thanks to the LORD, for his love endures forever," as Jehoshaphat led them into battle against a coalition of hostile nations (2 Chron. 20:21–22). We sing because it is part of our armor for battle in this life and the means of celebrating our victories—and in Christ, we always have the victory.

3. *The Songs of David*

The Psalms are songs that call us to sing. Honest, heartfelt, in desperation, in happiness, they teach us that since we are always saved, we are always able to sing:

> Praise the Lord, all nations. Glorify Him, all peoples. (Ps. 117:1 HCSB)

> Sing to the LORD, bless his name; tell of his salvation from day to day. (Ps. 96:2 ESV)

Sing to Him, sing praise to Him; tell about all His wonderful works. (Ps. 105:2)

Throughout the main songbook of the Bible, the Psalms, there is a regular pattern of revelation and response. Listen in to two:

1. Psalm 40—The psalmist looks to God to reveal Himself; God hears him, lifts him up, and gives him a firm place to stand . . . and puts a hymn of praise in his mouth.

> He lifted me out of the slimy pit,
>> out of the mud and mire;
> he set my feet on a rock
>> and gave me a firm place to stand.
> He put a new song in my mouth,
>> a hymn of praise to our God. (vv. 2–3)

2. Psalm 31—King David, the psalmist, sings of how he saw the goodness of the Lord in troubled times and then responded in praise.

> How abundant are the good things
>> that you have stored up for those who fear you,
> that you bestow in the sight of all,
>> on those who take refuge in you.
> In the shelter of your presence you hide them
>> from all human intrigues;
> you keep them safe in your dwelling
>> from accusing tongues.

> Praise be to the LORD,
>> for he showed me the wonders of his love
>> when I was in a city under siege. (vv. 19–21)

Meditating on who God is and all He has done triggers an authentic response of praise to God from our hearts and from our singing.

4. *The Songs of the Prophets*

The Israelites sang during Ezra's day when the foundation of the new temple was completed by the returning exiles (Ezra 3:10–13)—just as they sang when the walls were thoroughly rebuilt around Jerusalem under the leadership of Nehemiah (Neh. 12:27–29). They knew that it was God who had brought them back from exile, who had restored their hope and promised them future blessing. So they sang. Singing together marked both the rhythms of their daily life and the special occasions.

The prophets sang because of the salvation that they had seen, but more than that because of the salvation that they had foreseen. They told the people to sing of what they knew was coming—the Messiah, who would restore God's kingdom and His people: "Be joyful, rejoice together, you ruins of Jerusalem! For the LORD has comforted His people" (Isa. 52:9 HCSB). "Sing to the LORD! Praise the LORD, for He rescues the life of the needy from the hand of evil people" (Jer. 20:13 HCSB). "Sing aloud, O daughter of Zion; shout, O Israel. Rejoice and exult with all your heart" (Zeph. 3:14 ESV).

We join with them by singing about what they looked forward to, and we look back to: the coming of the Lord Jesus Christ, "for no matter how many promises God has made, they are 'Yes' in Christ. And so through him the 'Amen' is spoken by us to the glory of God" (2 Cor. 1:20).

5. *A Song That Sustains the Prisoners*

Salvation enables joy and compels singing even when circumstances are set dead against us. This is the wonder of gospel singing—since nothing can separate us from the love of God in Jesus Christ (Rom. 8:38–39), nothing need or can or should stop us singing. The early church was a singing church, even in the most difficult of circumstances. And so we find Paul and Silas, detained in a Philippian jail, facing a very uncertain tomorrow, but who could be heard at midnight "praying and singing hymns to God" (Acts 16:25). It strengthened them; it witnessed to the jailer, who, having heard the singing and witnessed the earthquake God sent, asked the apostles, "Sirs, what must I do to be saved?" (v. 30). They had clearly not been singing quietly under their breath! Salvation's songs are sung in any and every season of life.

I'M CLEAN, I'M CLEAN

We both grew up listening to the sounds of the Brooklyn Tabernacle Choir. There was a period in Kristyn's life when her dad would play a short film of the testimony of one of the choir members, Calvin Hunt, every morning before they headed out for the day. Calvin's life had been destroyed by crack cocaine and he had been living on the streets, estranged from his family, when he stumbled into Brooklyn Tabernacle Church one day, heard the gospel, and committed his life to Christ. The key moment in the interview was the one that showed him singing with the choir, his face shining and voice bursting with the lyrics:

There is a blood, a cleansing blood, that flows from
    Calvary
And in this blood there's a saving power
For it washes white and makes me clean
I'm clean, I'm clean, I've been washed in His blood.[9]

Calvin didn't need to be told to sing. Singing gives voice to a heart that deeply knows the gospel of grace. It is the overflow of a heart captivated by the gospel. In as many voices that join together to sing there are as many hearts that are called to know Christ as Lord and Savior. From that place there is a genuine and rich overflow of praise. This should reassure us. No matter how you are feeling, nor how good or bad a week you've had, you can lift your eyes to Jesus with relief, for He has washed you clean, and so you can sing wherever your life is at and whatever you are facing.

Calvin has now gone to be with the Lord. But he has not stopped singing. The book of Revelation paints a breathtaking, heaven-sent picture of angels, and saints, and indeed all creation, singing to the One upon the throne. Revelation 15 describes the saints as "they held harps given them by God and sang the song of God's servant Moses and of the Lamb" (v. 2)—the song of salvation Israel sang on the eastern shore of the Red Sea, that we sing when we gather today, and that all God's people through all the ages shall one day join together in His new creation to sing:

> Great and marvelous are your deeds,
> > Lord God Almighty.
> Just and true are your ways,
> > King of the nations.
> Who will not fear you, Lord,
> > and bring glory to your name?
> For you alone are holy.
> All nations will come
> > and worship before you,
> for your righteous acts have been revealed.
> (Rev. 15:3–4)

We will spend our eternity singing, for the gospel compels us to sing. And we are a people who, as we reflect on the gospel, cannot help but sing. We do not sing because we have to. We sing because we love to.

DISCUSSION QUESTIONS

1. If "worship is a response to revelation," what devotional practices in your own life might help you connect congregational singing as a response to freedom in Christ?

2. What psalm or other Scripture passage resonates with you as your "Song of Salvation"? Why?

3. What song would you consider to be your personal "testimony" song (as "I'm Clean" was for gospel singer Calvin Hunt—find a video of his performance online)?

We sing because we're created to, commanded to, and compelled to. And when we sing great truths, great things happen. Christ-filled, Spirit-prompted singing moves out in concentric circles changing your own heart and mind . . . changing your family . . . changing your church . . . and changing this world. These next four chapters will show you how.

CHAPTER 4

SING! . . . WITH HEART AND MIND

People say you are what you eat. Well, songs are food for the soul. What you sing, and don't sing, changes you.

Your heart and mind require a good, balanced diet of gospel truth that will build you up for your working week, your times of trial, and for each season of life. The lyrics of the songs we sing in our churches and repeat in our hearts find their way into shaping our priorities, our behavior, our loves . . . into the quiet space (or not so quiet, if you have kids) of the car journey on a Monday morning, into the language of our prayers as we fall asleep, into the answers we give "for the hope that [we] have" (1 Pet. 3:15). It always strikes us in church prayer meetings how often we hear people use phrases in their prayers that come straight from the hymns they sing.

The truth is that the songs we sing on Sunday stick with us—and so they shape us. It's been said, rightly, that you have the people when you have their songs, perhaps even more than their sermons. That's because truth soars on the air of a great melody. Just as food is not simply enjoyed just because it is edible, we don't enjoy songs just because they contain truth, but because they are artistically beautiful and satisfying—they captivate us in a deeper and more durable way. Such songs thrill our minds and hearts. We can't wait to sing them, and we never forget them.

Throughout the centuries the people of God have in huge measure learned their faith through what they sang together. Eat good soul food on a Sunday and you will find your soul growing and thriving through the week, and through your life. Here's how that happens.

1. SINGING TAKES SUNDAY'S TRUTHS INTO MONDAY

The songs we sing on Sunday provide the soundtrack for our week. Singing files away the messages the lyrics convey in our minds and hearts. If we don't sing about a particular truth, it's very likely we'll pray about it less and live with little thought of it. Christ-filled songs can help motivate us into a day when we would rather stay in bed than get up and face that chore or meeting or project. They support us when we lack courage and need to bolster our faith. They help us remember Scripture. They keep uprooting the weeds of worry and fear that tangle our feet and trip us up. They help us when we don't know how to explain the gospel to a friend, but recalling a lyric gives us the words. They comfort us when we are hit with something unexpected or tragic.

Every day we wake to the sound of two voices—the one of Wisdom and the one of folly; the voice of the Lord and the voice of this fallen world. The gospel that seemed so clear and true on Sunday morning can so easily be chipped away at, twisted a little, and devalued by the messages we hear through the week. Singing deep songs of the Lord keeps the right voice loudest in our ears. To take just one example: if we start to believe the popular ideas that "Humanity is getting better," or "With enough education, or therapy, or reasoned thought we can sort our problems," or "God helps those who help themselves," this song will place our feet back on gospel truth:

> *Nothing in my hand I bring*
> *Simply to the cross I cling*
> *Naked, come to Thee for dress*
> *Helpless, look to Thee for grace*
> *Foul, I to the fountain fly;*
> *Wash me Savior or I die*
> (Augustus Toplady, "Rock of Ages," 1763)

We need to sing over and over again of how we were once under the wrath of God, condemned to die, without even a hint of hope. We need to sing of how hope came from above, in human form, as the Son of God entered the world to provide a way for the salvation of all mankind. We need to sing of how . . .

> he made himself nothing
> by taking the very nature of a servant,
> being made in human likeness.
> And being found in appearance as a man,
> he humbled himself
> by becoming obedient to death—
> even death on a cross!
> Therefore God exalted him to the highest place
> and gave him the name that is above every name,
> that at the name of Jesus every knee should bow,
> in heaven and on earth and under the earth,
> and every tongue acknowledge that
> Jesus Christ is Lord,
> to the glory of God the Father. (Phil. 2:7–11)

Friends, if our singing is not impacting how we process life—if it is not strengthening us, training us, encouraging us, and comforting us, then we have not unwrapped the gift that singing is to us. We've been playing with the wrappings.

Most of us sing at times in our week, or hum a tune that reminds us of its lyrics. Be singing what you sang on Sunday. Be singing the gospel.

2. SINGING SUSTAINS YOU IN
EVERY SEASON OF LIFE

Since our songs are our soul food, if we desire to be spiritually healthy, then one of the key challenges is to work out how to cultivate a balanced and varied diet in the songs we regularly choose to sing—that is, the songs your church leaders choose to sing on a Sunday, and the songs you choose to sing through your week (whether you're listening to a playlist, whistling them in the shower, or whispering them under your breath as you go into a work meeting or a hospital appointment).

Close to our home on the North Irish coast there once lived a bishop's wife named Cecil Francis Alexander. Troubled by the lack of biblical knowledge and spiritual understanding of the children in and around their church, she began to write hymns for them to sing together, songs that would sow and water seeds of Bible truth into their young minds and hearts.

Although written more than one hundred years ago, you might know some of them: "All Things Bright and Beautiful" (on the theme of creation), "Once in Royal David's City" (the Christmas story), "There Is a Green Hill Far Away" (the crucifixion). Alexander understood that songs were not simply expressions of praise to punctuate a service or to entertain when attention was dwindling, but powerful tools in which beautiful truth set to memorable music could inspire deeper faith.

Today, Alexander's hymns are considered by many to be too heavy—for adults. Songs written for twentieth-century children to feast on are now thought too much for twenty-first-century *adults* to digest. That's an interesting commentary on our general approach to feeding our souls, particularly when you think that she was writing long before the hyper-communication of our technological age. Given the sheer quantity of information and messages that come at us each day (not to mention the growing hostility to the Christian faith in Western culture), the need to feed on what Paul called the "whole counsel of God" (Acts 20:27 ESV) through good songs that we can remember is surely, if anything, even greater than when she wrote those songs for young children.

If we are to be prepared to live for Christ in the whole of life, we need to be singing about the whole of life. In this, the only divinely authored hymnal in history is both our guide and our challenge. The Psalms are songs to God, about God, sung in community with the people of God. Through the centuries they have been the greatest source of inspiration for writing and singing hymns. The Psalms are our best resource for teaching us what to sing about, and how to apply the gospel to every season of life. Tim and Kathy Keller, in their excellent devotional on the Psalms, *The Songs of Jesus*, write that they "are not just a matchless primer of teaching but a medicine chest for the heart and the best possible guide for practical living."[10] So much could be said about the Psalms, but for the purposes of this short book we have highlighted just two ways they gave God's people centuries ago, and offer God's people still today, rich, varied food.

First, *the Psalms give us a vast vision of who God is.* "What ought to make worship delightful to us is not, in the first instance, its novelty or its aesthetic beauty, but its object. God Himself is delightfully wonderful, and we learn to delight in Him."[11] When you walk through the elegant halls of the National Portrait Gallery in London, you see the faces and contexts of countless people through history revealed through different colors, techniques, and details. Imagine the Psalms as a portrait gallery of God Himself. As we walk through them, we see portrait after portrait of His character displayed with different color and emphasis. He is the Judge, for whom perfect justice is intensely important (Ps. 75). He is the Shepherd, gathering us in and protecting us as lambs (Ps. 23). He is a holy God, for whom purity will never be compromised, so that only that which is pure can be in His presence (Ps. 15). He is King of all the earth and all the nations, and so He laughs at the arrogant scoffing of man (Ps. 2). He is Creator, and has written His Word into all He has made that we might see and know Him (Ps. 19).

There are psalms that describe His voice (Ps. 29), the attention He pays to our tears (Ps. 56) and to our burdens (Ps. 25). There are psalms that tell the glorious things He has done for His people (Ps. 78) and psalms that tell the glorious things He will one day do for us (Ps. 31).

The biggest difference between the Psalms and much of our modern music today is not (as many think) the length of songs, or the lack of repetition, or of the lesser use of the "I" pronoun—it is the breadth and depth of the character of God and how we as His creation humbly find our place within that. We are part of a victorious redemption history, present, and future—those who first sang the Psalms were reminded of that over and over again. We need to sing a diet that grows in us a confidence and a deepening joy of a God who is greater than we could ever imagine, and yet who loves us as His children more than we could ever imagine. For, of course, our eternal God is not locked in portraits from long ago or far removed from us—through the work of His Son and the presence of His Spirit, He comes to each of us in personal relationship and growing breadth of understanding. Sing and sing again songs that help you see God, so that you are moved to love Him more and transformed by His Spirit to become more and more like His Son.

Second, *the Psalms show us how to deal with real life.* Eugene Peterson writes that the Psalms are a place where we "find the experience of being human before God exposed and sharpened."[12] They awaken the mind and the affections of our hearts and reach into the fullness of human existence. They are incredibly honest, embracing the realities of life and singing through them. The Psalms take us from the wrenching lament of, "How long, LORD? Will you forget me forever?" (Ps. 13:1) to the leaping praise of, "My heart is glad and my tongue rejoices . . . because you will not abandon me to the realm of the dead" (Ps. 16:9–10); from the experience of having "feet like the feet of a deer; he causes me to stand on the heights" (Ps. 18:33) to those times when we know that "we are dust" (Ps. 103:14); and from the depths of those times when it seems God has "taken from me friend and neighbor—darkness is my closest friend" (Ps. 88:18) to the heights of knowing that He makes "known to me the path of life; you will fill me with joy in your presence, with eternal pleasures at your right hand" (Ps. 16:11).

Over a third of the Psalms can be categorized as laments. Over and over again these songs face up to the sharpest of pains, the deepest of struggles, and the loneliest of moments. As we prepare to lead church singing, we often remember Henry David Thoreau's words: "The mass of men lead lives of quiet desperation."[13] This is where many of us are as we gather together on a Sunday. Through the course of our lives, we may well know times when it's easy to have a spring in our step as we stand to sing; but often we come to sing with heaviness of heart, where our singing chokes a little in our souls, if not in our throats. None of us comes with everything figured out. We need to have songs that recognize these realities without leaving us to despair of those realities, because they lead us to the Rock that is higher than us.

Someone who has always inspired us by her example of faith through suffering is Joni Eareckson Tada. She once wrote, "My weakness, that is, my quadriplegia, is my greatest asset because it forces me into the arms of Christ every single morning when I get up."[14] One of the ways she has done this is to sing. We can't remember a time being with Joni where she didn't lead those people around her in singing. She loves to sing of the gospel, loves singing songs old and new, and loves to sing of heaven in particular. Over the decades since, singing with believers has helped sustain her like nothing else. One hymn that is a particular favorite of Joni's is "Abide with Me":

> *Abide with me; fast falls the eventide;*
> *The darkness deepens; Lord with me abide.*
> *When other helpers fail and comforts flee,*
> *Help of the helpless, O abide with me.*
> (Henry Francis Lyte, 1847)

If our songs are not giving us a balanced, rich, nutritious diet, we will not be spiritually healthy people. It seems to us that in years past people went back to church when they were struggling, whether it was with the loss of a family member, ailing health, or a lack of rain for the crops. In church, they found a realism about life as it is now, and a hope for the life to come. Could it be that many of our services today turn people off who are suffering and seeking Christ? Do our songs present a veneer of happiness rather than a robust joy in the midst of pain? Are the fountains we point to as we sing deep enough to meet the thirst that the trials of life give us? If not, then our diet is impoverished—our words are too small.

The Psalms tell us to sing when we're happy. We have freedom to dance with exuberance, to shout loudly, to sing and play music with artistic excellence, to celebrate our victories. But we must not *only* sing songs that help us when we're happy. We can also sing because we're sad, and we must also sing of Christ when we're sad. We have freedom to weep, to pour out our souls to a God who hears and who acts. We sing for our brothers and sisters in those moments or seasons when they cannot. We sing, as the Psalms train us, to help us bring all of our lives, failures, successes, losses, gains, dreams, and ambitions into gospel perspective. Our singing can prepare us for every season of life, and sustain us through every season of life. We don't need a musical escape from our lives; we need to gaze on the Savior of our lives—our refuge and help and comfort.

3. SINGING REMINDS YOU OF WHAT GOD HAS DONE IN YOUR LIFE

Many of us can probably think of a hymn or song we sang a long time ago that still holds influence on us today. One such song for us is "Great Is Thy faithfulness," written in the 1920s. It was sung forty years ago at Kristyn's parents wedding. We remember singing it as kids, then as teenagers, and during our university years as we worked through the questions and doubts we all bring as we consider our faith. As newlyweds and then as new parents we sang it together, looking at those older than us who once faced what we did now. As they sang, "All I have needed Thy hands hath provided," it encouraged us that God was and is and would be faithful to us as He had been to them. We've watched one of our daughters stand and sing it with her grandparents and thought of how this beautiful song might follow her on her own journey of faith.

Great is Thy faithfulness, O God my Father;
there is no shadow of turning with Thee;
Thou changest not, Thy compassions, they fail not;

as Thou hast been Thou forever will be.
Great is Thy faithfulness. Great is Thy faithfulness.
Morning by morning new mercies I see;
all I have needed Thy hand hath provided;
great is Thy faithfulness, Lord, unto me.
(Thomas Chisolm, 1923)

Some of us can remember the first Christian song we sang after putting our faith in Jesus. Some of us were singing at the very moment that we put our faith in Him. Some of us can mark a moment when God was very close to lead us through a tragedy by way of a song. Others can remember pouring out praise in a moment of great joy. And when we sing those songs again, it's an opportunity to be encouraged and excited and humbled all over again—to remember that great is God's faithfulness . . . that every morning has provided new mercies . . . that all we have needed His hand has provided. As you remember God's faithfulness in your past, so often etched in your hearts through a song, you are inspired and equipped to face the ups and downs of the week. This is one of the reasons you need a good amount of good songs stored up to carry with you through all of your life.

4. SINGING KEEPS YOUR MIND ON ETERNITY

One night as our daughter Eliza climbed into bed she said, "Mom, sing that song about how 'Soon oh very soon we are going to see the King.' Do you know that one?"

Yes, we know that one.

Our true joy is squeezed out if the content of our singing becomes too bookended by the short stretch of our life on earth. We need our singing to be filled with the unending story of the hope of heaven and its very real presence through the moments of everyday life.

We also look to our singing to remind us of what is the comfort to God's people but the anguish of those outside His grace—God's judgment and the eternal lostness of all those who die refusing to trust in the Lord for their salvation. Yet, probably as a reaction to the "fire and brimstone" preaching of a previous generation, we have perhaps swung too much the other way. In one recently published hymnbook we read through, out of more than 150 songs, only three focused on heaven, hell, judgment, or that we are eternal beings.

After all, one day we will sing our last song in this life, and the realities of life beyond death will be our present experience. Let the songs your church sings now that speak to you of eternity be so familiar to you that they are in your heart and on your lips as you enter eternity.

Keith's grandfather used to arrive at Sunday worship a good forty-five minutes early. He would sit down in the place where he always sat and would flip through his hymnal and pray as he prepared for the service. Those songs held him. They taught him. They rehearsed the truth for him. They kept him looking forward to what was eternally real—what had always been true from before the foundation of the world, and what would remain being true for the rest of his lifetime and beyond. And when he was in his nineties, and was unable to remember his own family's names, much less accomplish even the most basic, everyday task, he could still recite or respond to the words and melodies of those hymns.

Those were the songs he had sung and carried with him throughout his life. Locked inside the folds and wrinkles of his long-term memory, he was able to retrieve them when everything else had become confused. And they brought him considerable peace, even at the most difficult stages of his declining years. For him, as for many, life's greatest battles were at the end. He had his songlist for that time prepared, and it carried him into glory. Like him, we need to sing the songs now that we want to grow old with—songs that will lift our hearts and sights to eternity and our eternal Lord when earthly life begins to slip from our hands. Like him, we need to sing those songs with others in our churches, that they, too, may look to eternity every day, including their last day. May we, like him, fall asleep with gospel songs on our lips and awake to the sounds of heaven singing.

SCALLOPS AND SINGING

When we lived in Ohio, there was a restaurant we loved in Hudson where you could sit close to the kitchen and watch and talk to the chefs as they were cooking. Keith had never really tasted scallops before, and hadn't thought much about eating scallops before, and wasn't keen on the idea, but as the chef cooked them in the right way, talked through the process, and let him taste some, he found that he liked them. Then he found he loved them. Soon enough, he discovered that this restaurant had changed his palate forever.

You need to grow your appetite for good soul food—for congregational singing. You grow it through focus, and by follow-up. When you are in church, and you stand to sing, consciously focus on what is going on, so that your attention does not flicker. When we sing, it is not that God suddenly arrives (He is in all places, at all times). He is never absent—but very often, we are. (We've all found ourselves thinking about a work issue or mentally preparing a shopping list while everyone else around us is singing.) Ask God to help you focus; think about the words you are singing and the images they are painting; respond in prayer to lines that particularly strike you; be mindful of those around you, enjoying being part of something greater than just yourself; make a note of any words or phrases you don't understand, to ask your pastor or another Christian later. If you find your attention has, after all, flickered, don't give up—refocus.

And then, once you are into your week, follow up by singing the songs. Remember them as you wake in the morning, as you stand in the shower, as you drive to work, as you exercise in the gym, as you go about your work, as you spend time with your family, and as you fall asleep at night. Put song lists together that you can listen to and sing along to. Keep a hymnal or notes with lyrics on them with your

Bible. Sing to yourself what you sang on Sunday, for what you sing shapes your heart, your mind, your soul. Give yourself good, deep, rich, gospel truth to feed on. You are what you sing.[15]

DISCUSSION QUESTIONS

1. Is there a hymn, or hymns, from your past that acts as a "milestone marker" for your walk with Christ? Why is it still significant and how does it speak to your heart today?

2. What modern song (new to you in the past few years) has connected with you in such a way that you believe it may become a "milestone" hymn for you in the future?

3. Do your favorite songs that you love to sing give a broad and deep picture of the character and nature of God? Can the same be said of how we think about God and how we pray to Him?

4. Do the songs we sing connect us to every season of life (seasons of suffering and aging as well as celebrations and times of thanksgiving)?

5. How much do we lean on hymns we sing in church throughout the week (in the morning, in the car, at work)?

CHAPTER 5

SING! . . . WITH YOUR FAMILY

Love the LORD your God with all your heart and
with all your soul and with all your strength. These
commandments that I give you today are to be on your
hearts. Impress them on your children. Talk about them
when you sit at home and when you walk along the road,
when you lie down and when you get up. (Deut. 6:5–7)

Taking this command seriously includes singing the songs of our faith in the home. In *your* home. The church should be a feasting place for singable songs, and the appetite for it is nurtured at home.

It was a Puritan practice back in the seventeenth century that a man would be refused communion on a Sunday if he was not actively and consistently involved in leading prayer and singing and Bible study with his family during the week. We are not suggesting reviving that approach! But if our spiritual forefathers took what happened in the home so seriously, shouldn't we, too?

We know that singing at home may be an idea that makes *you* feel uncomfortable. Maybe you are thinking right now:

But my kids don't want to hear my singing voice.

But my kids won't want to join in.

But I can't play any instruments.

But what would we sing?

If that's you, this chapter will give you fresh perspective. If this is something you already do regularly, we hope this chapter will encourage you and give you some ideas.

Just a quick word before we start: the focus here is on family, on homes that include children. If that's not your home at the moment, do think about how the principles here relate to where you are in life right now, or where you might one day find yourself. At the very least, they can help you pray well for the families in your church, which is no bad thing!

SINGING AND SKIING

In traditional Irish culture, stories of heroes and the values that they shared were often passed on through song. As we grew up, it was a familiar sight to see families and friends singing together in homes and small public spaces, reinforcing the sense of community and shared experience through their music. More than listening to a soloist, or reciting a chant at a sports match, or holding a once-a-year Christmas carol sing-along, in these familiar and organic contexts children found their singing voices and learned their culture.

Parents in ancient Israel were also charged with making sure their kids learned their culture, which included learning the truths about the God of Israel. The clear, unflinching cry of the Shema (quoted earlier) rang out to the ear of every parent. And one of the ways they "impressed" the truth on their children was through the songs they sang with them—songs like:

> I will open my mouth with a parable;
>> I will utter hidden things, things from of old—
> things we have heard and known,
>> things our ancestors have told us.
> We will not hide them from their descendants;
>> we will tell the next generation
> the praiseworthy deeds of the LORD,
>> his power, and the wonders he has done.
> (Ps. 78:2–4)

Our culture is different, but the charge is the same. If you are a Christian parent, you stand in that line and you have that responsibility. We live in a performance culture, where experts play and we listen, but we and our children are missing out on something hugely significant if this is all music is to us, and particularly to our kids. Sally Goddard Blythe, a British consultant in neuro-developmental education, wrote in *The Genius of Natural Childhood*, "Song is a special type of speech. Lullabies, songs and rhymes of every culture carry the 'signature' melodies and inflections of a mother tongue, preparing a child's ear, voice and brain for language."[16] In other (simpler!) words, singing is one of the best ways to teach kids, and we should start when they are young.

When we were first married we lived in Geneva, Switzerland, for one year. We discovered a love for skiing (which unfortunately never loved us back—we were both terrible at it). We often found ourselves crawling down a slope while trying to stay out of the way of several little children who were flying past us. We asked our Swiss friends at what age they had learned to ski, and one girl said to us that she didn't remember learning, because she was so young when she started. That same girl had also spoken several other languages flawlessly since her "wee years"—they were second nature to her, because she learned them as a little child.

Let singing the gospel be to your family what skiing incredibly early and speaking multiple languages is to the Swiss. We need to make singing Bible truths second nature to our children, a "second language" in our homes. Sing about those truths when you sit at home and when you walk along the road, when you lie down, and when you get up. Sing with your kids as you put them to bed at night, or you sit down for dinner, or as you drive in the car with a CD on. Sooner or later, they'll start singing unprompted. Join in with them.

Since we have had kids and tried to get to grips with parenting, we've frequently asked older parents the "How did you do it?" question. Keith once asked Dr. John MacArthur this question. He said that as he and his wife looked back on those formative years of raising their family, their high-priority habit of immersing their children in Word-filled memorable music was key. He recounted how they'd always tried to fill as many different parts of their lives as possible with opportunities for singing, playing tapes and then CDs in the car, in the kitchen, in the living room, in their bedrooms at night.

MEMORABLE UNDERSTANDING

Songs help us train children in the "language" of the Christian faith. What we want to teach our kids travels deeper inside them when we sing it rather than only speak it to them.

In Exodus 12, as God gives Moses instructions for how Israelite families are to celebrate the Passover each year to remember their rescue from Egypt, He says:

> "And when your children ask you, 'What does this ceremony mean to you?' then tell them, 'It is the Passover sacrifice to the LORD . . ." (vv. 26–27)

Retellings of history in the Old Testament did not exclude the children; neither did the Psalms. And that little phrase "and when your children ask you" is very telling. First, your faith must be evident enough that a child asks questions about it. Second, you need to be prepared to give answers to your children. Of course, our Passover meal is the Lord's Supper. But this principle applies more broadly, too. Singing together in the home is an excellent way to prompt questions and give answers and aim for depth of spiritual understanding in our children in a memorable way:

> "What does 'when with the ransomed in glory' mean, Mom?"
> or
>
> "Why would you want a thousand tongues to sing, Dad?"

Singing the gospel changes hearts, and singing the gospel prepares hearts. Singing is of course not a magical formula that will guarantee deep faith in a child, but it is a way to sow and water the Word of God in their heart. If a child does walk through a rebellious season, what do you want them to remember about the Christian faith, calling and inviting them back? Fill their memories up now with the gospel, through songs that will keep singing to them through the years to come.

While our faith must be taught, it is also "caught" in our homes, through what our kids see and hear from us. And singing is catchy. So sing with your kids. You don't need to be able to sing well. Our singing always remains more important than the sound it makes.

WHAT SHOULD CHILDREN SING?

When he was working out how to write stories for children, C. S. Lewis was guided by what he liked himself. Songs are the same. Sing what *you* like, what you enjoy singing, the songs that are good for your spiritual well-being. At the heart of encouraging your kids to sing is having a heart for singing the songs yourself.

In an essay on writing for children, Lewis also suggested that children don't learn like a train going from station to station but rather as a tree grows by adding rings. Kids add and build on what they already know, and so do adults; so we must take care to try and make those first key rings of growth healthy and strong, providing a solid foundation a child can build on. We consider the balance of the content they sing and what vision of God those songs are growing in their minds.

As parents of young children, we are learning not to patronize them or underestimate what they learn and retain through what they sing. With our kids we have always sung simple songs like "Jesus Loves Me," but also longer, fuller hymns on the same subject like "How Deep the Father's Love for Us." Don't be afraid of the older hymns containing "Thees" and "Thous," but explain them as you need to. Kristyn's great-grandmother would often recite "Jesus tender Shepherd hear me, bless Thy little lamb tonight" before she and her sister would go to sleep. It didn't confuse them but rather helped tune their ear to the poetry of hymns.

We can give children a little more than they understand in the songs we sing with them, and over time help them grow into an understanding of every part of a lyric, just like buying new shoes for your kid a size bigger than they need right now, so that they grow into them and get longer wear out of them. Equally, don't underestimate the value of songs that tell great Bible stories or help with memorizing Bible verses (but be discerning—just because the tune is catchy and your kids enjoy singing a song, does not mean it has helpful lyrics).

BUT MY KIDS ARE TEENAGERS . . .

Perhaps you are reading this and thinking, *My kids are older, and this is not what our home has been like. How do I start singing with teens?*

Since we are not there yet, we asked a parent who had a home where both teenagers and singing were present at the same time! You might be familiar with Bobbie Wolgemuth. She and Joni Eareckson Tada wrote a series of books called *Hymns for a Kid's Heart* telling the stories behind the hymns and teaching the hymns themselves. Bobbie did not grow up in a Christian family, and when she had her own kids, she and her husband, Robert, made a conscious decision that they would fill their home with hymns of faith. The kids sang as teenagers, as part of the fabric of life, like while helping their mom make dinner. Bobbie passed away from cancer several years ago, and these hymns she learned as a new believer and then as a mother sustained her through her illness. When we asked Robert about singing with teenagers, he made a few suggestions:

1. Tell and show your kids why this is important. Be part of a church family that enables you to clearly show congregational singing done well, especially with opportunities where you can sing with your kids in church and not always send them away to another service just for them.
2. Make it as fun and attractive to them as possible. Find contemporary versions of good songs that appeal to a teenager's ear.
3. Get started. Start playing songs in your home. Let them see you singing.
4. Don't be scared of your kids. You have the right and responsibility to parent them.

We have noticed many times that when parents, and particularly fathers, do not sing, it often leads to older kids inheriting similar tepid responses that sadly often go far beyond just the singing. Be a parent who sings with joy, and pray that your kids, of whatever age, would follow you—not just in the singing, but in the faith that brings such joy.

THE SOUND OF HOME IN CHURCH

These "at home" experiences are foundational spaces for the singing we do from Sunday to Sunday. It links our personal homes with our church home, training kids to sing and sing well as part of the congregation. It links our homes to our kids' future homes, training this generation how to one day sing with their children. It helps prepare our kids and us for our eternal home when all the families of the world will join in praise of the Savior.

We believe that singing is transformative. In a culture where the bonds of family are often brittle, singing together can put strength in our arms as we hold on to each other. It can help restore how God intends family to be, linking us in where there is pressure to pull away. It can train us to be comfortable and confident in speaking of our faith and not unfamiliar and shy. And, if you are disheartened by the trends of music in the wider church at the moment, remember: some of the people who will write the songs, choose the songs, and lead the singing in churches tomorrow are in our care and training today. If we can inspire joyful, thoughtful, heartfelt Christian singing in our homes today, we can transform the Church in a single generation. What an opportunity!

Friends, let's take singing within our families seriously, as an investment in our kids' spiritual health:

People and realms from every tongue
Dwell on His love with sweetest song

And infant voices shall proclaim
Their early blessings of His name.
(Isaac Watts, "Jesus Shall Reign," 1719)

TEN PRACTICAL IDEAS

As young parents of three young girls, we are amateurs when it comes to parenting (who isn't?!). Most of these ideas for getting kids singing the gospel we have admired in and copied from other families.

1. Use All the Help and Opportunities You Can Get

Sing yourself as you go around your home. Stream the songs from Sunday during breakfast, or over your smartphone during part of the bedtime routine. If your kids are learning to play instruments, get hymn sheet music. Ask your children what songs they enjoy singing in church and sing them at home. We are not saying that your home should sound as though Maria Von Trapp took up residence there. But aim to have truth being sung in the spaces where life takes place. Keith's family regularly sang the blessing before a meal, and we now do the same with our kids. For example, Calvin's Doxology, "Praise God from whom all blessings flow," which is a wonderful Trinitarian lyric for kids to sing.

2. Teach Your Kids Songs You Want Them to Grow Old With

Actively make a list of the songs you would like your kids to know throughout their lives, that clearly and richly teach the faith. Then play them in the car and around the house; sing them yourself as you go about your day, and draw attention to them when they are sung on a Sunday. The best songs for our youth are often the best songs for our old age.

3. Talk about What You're Doing and What the Songs Mean

Take time to talk about why we sing, what happens when we sing, and how we use the gift of singing to serve one another.

One of the funniest things is to hear your kids mispronounce lyrics, because they don't know what a word means. Take a moment to draw attention to a word or phrase that you could explain. Use a lyric as a conversation starter about faith. We teach our girls a hymn of the month. When we learned "Holy, Holy, Holy," we had some fun with cherubims and seraphims! We recommend Joni Eareckson Tada and Bobbie Wolgemuth's series *Hymns for a Kid's Heart* for helping with this.

4. Prepare for Sunday Services

Before we had kids, we had no idea what a major achievement it is just to get the whole family out to church on time on a Sunday! But when you can, help your kids to sing on a Sunday in church by singing the songs as a family beforehand. This means they'll know the tune, understand the more complex words or concepts, and be able to sing with confidence and joy. There are few sights more lovely than the expression on the face of a young child who has just realized he or she knows the words to the next song being sung in their church. There are few sounds more wonderful than hearing a young child belt out those words in church (perhaps to a slightly different tune!) because they know the words.

Equally, it's great to chat about or sing the songs from church later on a Sunday. Most of us drive to and from church—a great time to talk, pray, and sing together about what we're about to do, and what we have just done. (We've found Bob Kauflin's insights on preparing your family for Sunday in the book *Worship Matters* very helpful.)

5. Model Passionate Participation in the Services

Always remember when you sing at church, your children (and everyone else's around you) can see you and are watching. We both have strong memories of watching our parents and grand-parents singing in church and valuing what they were doing. It's a wonderful thing to stand beside your children and sing with them. Children also need to see other parents, and kids older than them, singing, so that they see it is not a "childish" thing to do, and neither is it just some strange trait that only your family does! Sit somewhere in your church building where your kids are surrounded by strong singing. Use the songs of the church to help strengthen their vocal muscles and by extension their faith muscles too.

Grow the love for hearing and joining the voice of the congregation, so much so that church would be strange to them if they didn't hear that sound. They should come to church expecting to sing.

6. Be Aware of All the Music Your Kids Are Into

Keith has a vivid memory growing up of a school-friend's mother hearing of a new friend her child had made and asking him, "What are his friends like and what music is he into?" What an interesting question! It may seem somewhat simplistic and judgmental (and it may have been)—but it gets at the truth that music—all music—affects us as we listen. There are ultimately no neutral lyrics. All songs share a message about how we should view the world. So we should be listening, discussing, and understanding what our kids are into. It's not that we ban everything that does not explicitly teach the gospel! We love and play all sorts of music with our kids. But we want to equip our kids to listen with discernment and thoughtfulness.

7. If Your Kids Are into Music . . .

Encourage them! If they have a gift for music, help them to see that it's given them by the Lord, for using to serve the Lord's people (Eph. 4:7–8, 12). The church is (and has been throughout history) an incredible breeding ground for musical training and expression.

We both grew up with parents who not only drove us all over for music lessons and rehearsals, but had homes with "open doors"—four long-suffering parents who, as we began making music, opened their homes for eating and meeting, rehearsing and discussing, celebrating and commiserating. If your kids are musical, then be those parents. It's tiring, but it's also joyful!

8. If Your Church Has a Children's Choir, Support It If You Can

In the busyness of life this can feel like yet another thing, another carpool journey (more time to play music though!). It's an encouragement to the children—it will draw them into life-long singing in the church and they will learn to be singers. It's an encouragement to a whole congregation—when kids sing it has a very special impact on people listening (Ps. 8:2). One of the reasons we began our "Kids Hymnal" series was hearing kids sing inspires other kids, and the grown-ups, to sing.

9. Cultivate High Opinions of All Types of Art

Some of the issues in church music today are not that a certain style isn't quite right but rather that we are too narrow and maybe even too boring in our expression. Inspire your kids with different instruments, sounds, and languages, and by speaking positively about all these things yourself. Teach them to be life-long students of discovery in this amazing creation God has built all around us and in us.

In the Getty and Lennox households, we both benefited from lively artistic discussions on classical music, books, travel, and faith that encouraged curiosity, sincerity, and creativity.

10. Sing Today

There may never be a perfect day to start singing truths with your kids. But there is today. They are not too old. They are not too young—we have been surprised that even our two-year-old knows several songs well. (Remember the ancient motto—"Give me a child until they are seven and I will show you the man.") Don't wait. We were kick-started into this by a hilarious experience at Wilberforce School (New Jersey) when the kids wanted to perform one of our songs (they began by explaining how they used different hymns to help teach the kids the faith), and our daughter Eliza (four at the time) jumped up to join the choir and of course, was the only child who didn't know all the words—an embarrassing parenting moment!

Think of one or two things you need to change, and get started, and keep going. Sing together today.

DISCUSSION QUESTIONS

1. If you grew up in a Christian home, what songs from your childhood do you most remember? What hymns do you know? What Bible verses and stories do you know because of songs? What hymns do you want to pass down to your children?

2. If you are a parent or grandparent, how do you feel singing to and with your children or grandchildren? Can you think of ways to make it easy, fun, and a natural part of family life?

3. What parts of church do children and teenagers currently enjoy? What can we do to make singing in church more engaging and enjoyable for children and teenagers?

4. What is holding your family back today from more singing in the home?

CHAPTER 6

SING! . . . WITH THE LOCAL CHURCH

The Giant's Causeway is a world heritage site minutes away from our front door in Northern Ireland. It is a geological marvel, consisting of forty thousand naturally occurring and mostly hexagonally shaped rocks, joined together at varying heights and rising up beside the wild Antrim coastline. Through many different weathers (most frequently rain) people come from all over the world to climb on the rocks and look out onto the waves.

There is something church-like about the sight. Peter writes in his first letter to the early church, "As you come to him, the living Stone—rejected by humans but chosen by God and precious to him—you also, like living stones, are being built into a spiritual house to be a holy priesthood, offering spiritual sacrifices acceptable to God through Jesus Christ" (1 Pet. 2:4–5).

Like these multi-angled stones, even with our sharp points and rough edges we who are God's people are being built together upon the solid Rock that is our Lord Jesus. The church is the only structure that will stand forever. Nothing—not even the very storms of hell—will prevail over it. Today, as you read, people from every nation, tribe, and tongue are coming to take refuge from the waves, just as we have done.

TOGETHER

The best most perfect way that we have of expressing a sweet concord of mind to each other is by music.[17]

When we sing together as the Church, we are showing how we are a congregation of living stones. Our singing is an audible expression of the bonds we share, testifying to the life that lies within these stones. We are cut from the same elements of faith, united in one Lord, filled by one Spirit, brought into one Church, to offer our praise to Him. We are being chiseled and refined through our singing, just as we are through every aspect of our lives. We are forged together through our singing together.

In many ways, the key word in that last sentence was not about music, nor even singing, but rather *together*. We live in a time when the importance of music in church has been elevated greatly (not least because it has become commercially lucrative). But at the same time, we are in danger of lowering the importance we place on singing *together*. Listening to each other mumbling quietly along as a band performs brilliantly on stage in a church building is not the same as singing together as a congregation. The medieval church made the error of treating the Lord's Supper as something for the congregation to watch as the professionals at the front participated. Might we not be in danger of doing the same with our music today?

So many of the instructions given to God's people are to be worked out in community, *together*. Strong, heartfelt congregational singing is a striking expression of this, of the Holy Spirit at work amongst us, and through us, as we sing of the very things we share as Christ's people.

So when you sing, look around. Encourage others with what you are singing, and expect to be encouraged by the fact that there are others singing with you and to you. All our individual stories meet at the cross-section of the worship service. We are reminded that we are not alone—we are members of a multi-generational, multi-ethnic, multi-*everything* family. We are reminded that we are not self-sufficient, for we need a Savior. We are reminded that we need not despair, for we have His Spirit within us. We are reminded that we are not the center of the universe, but just one voice and heart among the great worldwide throng of people praising the One who is. And we remind each other of all this as we sing *together.*

There is a family Kristyn has known since she was a little girl. The mom has been in a wheelchair for decades as a result of suffering with MS. When the congregation is asked to stand and sing, she has often held her husband's hand so she can express her desire to stand up with everyone through him. May your approach be the same as hers—that, spiritually speaking, even if you cannot do it physically, you are singing because you are standing together, on a firm foundation:

The Church's one foundation
is Jesus Christ her Lord;
she is His new creation
by water and the word:
from heaven He came and sought her
to be His holy bride;
with His own blood He bought her,
and for her life He died.
(Samuel Johnstone, "The Church's One Foundation," 1866)

NO MAN IS AN ISLAND

Nothing dilutes a congregation's singing or undermines our unity faster than forgetting this truth: we are not islands. Today there is a disturbing amount of believers who are drifting away from the habit of gathering weekly with other Christians in a local church. It's a result of seeing our faith as something individualistic and only personal, between us and God, with church there simply to serve that pursuit. It leads to people leaving churches because "I'm getting nothing out of it." Of course you should be personally benefiting from a local church—but you benefit from church only as you serve church. More often than not this sentiment thinly veils an excuse to skip the cost of commitment to community. We should never have been in church merely or primarily for what we get out of it, but what we give to it. The idea of "me" cannot be understood properly without the understanding of "us," of the church together.

Think about the churches to whom Paul was writing in the decades after Christ's ascension. Each was an eclectic collection of tastes, experiences, and backgrounds. They contained both the educated and the unschooled, those with plenty in their pockets and those struggling to make ends meet. They came from a variety of religious and cultural backgrounds, with many resulting tensions. They were susceptible to the vicious winds of false teaching and exposed to the waves of persecution that had begun to sweep through the Roman Empire. They had nothing in common, except that they had everything that mattered in common: faith in Christ, who joined them by His Spirit. And Paul told them that a sign of this would be seen in their congregational singing:

> . . . be filled with the Spirit, speaking to one another with psalms, hymns, and songs from the Spirit. Sing and make music from your heart to the Lord, always giving thanks to God the Father for everything, in the name of our Lord Jesus Christ. (Eph. 5:18–20)

Their songs were the flagpoles they could rally around. And it is just the same today. Hopefully, your church includes members who are very different than you—and who have very different musical tastes than you. Singing as one united church body reminds us all that we are not defined by the rugged individualism promoted by modern society. To "keep the unity of the Spirit" (Eph. 4:3) was a hard thing to do in the first century and required "every effort" from every church member; it's *still* a hard thing today, it still requires effort from you, and it still finds its expression and its inspiration in a church's gospel-fueled singing. We all share the responsibility of our singing together. Our singing (even when it joyfully falls off pitch) should always, unapologetically, contribute to our sense of family and community and never be rushed through, mumbled through, or handed over to the "professionals."

So when you are called to sing at church, stop drinking your coffee for a moment, put your phone away, and look around and listen to the people standing about you. You are not an only child. This is your family. You and these folk around you are the only eternal pieces of this fading world. You are called to serve them by singing with and to them.

When we see our singing together in this way, we will happily compromise when it comes to the style of the music, the instruments used in the music, and so on. Of course we'll find particular hymns and arrangements more to our own tastes, but there is something bigger and so much more exciting happening here. Don't view singing with church as an opportunity to sing in a way that sounds like the culture you live in, or like a past era you wish you lived in—come to sing to lend your voice to the timeless, boundless sound of the congregational voice singing to the One who is eternally worthy of our praise.

SINGING AND RECLAIMING
THE MILLENNIAL GENERATION

Most churches are painfully and personally aware of the significant drop-out of late teens and twenty-somethings from church, and often from Christian faith altogether. David Kinnaman, the president of the research company Barna Group, writes in his book *You Lost Me*: "The ages eighteen to twenty-nine are the black hole of church attendance."[18]

Understanding why is a complex question with many answers, but we have regularly wondered what part our approach to music in church has played in this—and not in the direction you might imagine. It may seem obvious that to draw the millennial generation back to church, what is needed is more of a gig- or concert-like atmosphere to our singing, rather than a congregational approach. After all, that's what they expect outside of the Church.

We want to suggest that our churches need to do *the exact opposite.* Back in chapter 2, we highlighted three aspects of being created in God's image that our singing together showcases—creativity, communication, and community. And that is what millennials (even all of us) are searching for . . .

Creativity. Creative types know that simplicity is often the highest form of creativity. Just look around at the design of everything from Apple products to cars. Given that the standard of production and use of technology are extremely high in so much we digest outside of church services, it is often the most simple thing done well and sincerely in church that will make the most significant impression. A stunning melody with clear and moving lyrics, sung with gusto and authenticity by a congregation, is a more powerful statement than a song that's difficult to play or is awkward for the congregation to sing. Gordon Ramsay, the outspoken chef from the UK, is famous for resuscitating a struggling restaurant by getting rid of an over-long, over-ambitious, unfocused menu and pairing it down to half a dozen meals they can cook well. A similar approach to the singing in church might be welcome, not just to the musicians, but also to those who are seeking creative simplicity and authenticity.

Communication. Are we communicating a deep faith through what we sing and how we sing it, or are we entertaining teenagers with something that will not hold water when they hit college or head out into the workplace? Kinnaman writes, "Without a clear path to pursue the true gospel, millions of young Christians will look back on their twenty-something years as a series of lost opportunities for Christ."[19] Biblically rich content in songs, sung by people who look like they mean what they are saying, helps teach the gospel as something that is credible and powerful rather than cultural and optional.

Community. Kinnaman asks, "Can the church rediscover the intergenerational power of the assembly of saints?"[20] We live in an increasingly fragmented age, where social media creates niches in which we can live without ever hearing from or thinking about the perspective of anyone older than us, younger than us, who is different than us, or disagrees with us. We are more connected than ever before, and lonelier than ever before. And our churches are often, sadly, not so different. We are whisked from the baby room to the toddler room, to children's church and then on to student ministry, to a church full of college students, and so it goes. A church that sings together—across generations, standing side by side, putting community unity before personal preferences—is making a powerful and attractive statement to those who yearn for community more authentic than can be enjoyed online and friendship deeper than is found in counting your Facebook friends.

SINGING SHAPES OUR LEGACY

Antoni Gaudi, the great Spanish architect, laid the first stone of his Sagrada Família cathedral in Barcelona, Spain, in 1882. It is due to be completed by 2026, by which point construction will have taken *144 years*. Gaudi died long ago without seeing its completion, and many others have added their expertise to his. But his cathedral will stand as an enduring legacy. He has left something beautiful behind.

Our generation of God's people will leave our songs behind. Our singing casts a light after we are gone. We each bear responsibility in the singing legacy we leave behind us. We should sing with a mind toward those younger than us who are listening in and learning from us. Someone took the time to share hymns of faith with us and we are to be faithful in doing the same. Every new generation needs its songs for the moment, but we also look for songs worth keeping that we can carry with us through all our moments to connect the pieces of our life to a steady rhythm that marks the short years we are given.

How we sing, what we sing, what we keep, and what we leave out are shaping the faith we hand on to the next generation and the musical heritage they will have. May it not be on our watch that good congregational singing is taken from or given away by the congregation, or that we do not carefully watch over what we sing.

WHICH KIND OF CHURCH?

Every time you sing, you are expressing something about what kind of a church you want to be, and what kind of church member you are going to be.

When we were a young newly married couple, fresh "off the boat" from Ireland, we were invited by a friend to sing at a Pentecostal church in Cambridge, just outside of Boston, Massachusetts. It was the sort of experience we had always dreamed of. A small New England congregation, an energetic preacher, lots of response from the people, incredible gospel harmonies, an amazing band. We sang "The Power of the Cross":

This the power of the cross
Christ became sin for us
Took the blame, bore the wrath
We stand forgiven at the cross.[21]

When we finished, the worship leader came forward and sang the chorus again, and some people came forward to accept Christ. Then the pastor stepped forward, spoke a little, and then sang the chorus again. Then the congregation sang another chorus. And we will never forget it. The passion. The community. The common joy of the gospel expressed in different ways, with different accents and expressions from our own. That is the power of the cross being expressed through the power of congregational singing.

Last year, we visited a beautiful cathedral in the middle of Ireland. It is in the center of the town and has been there for hundreds of years. But those walls that have echoed so much congregational singing now are filled with music for cultural events and fund-raisers for building maintenance. There is still music, and it may well be high-quality music that is enjoyable to listen to. But it is not Christian congregational singing. And that is a tragedy.

Which church would you like yours to resemble in a century? Not all singing churches are healthy churches, but all healthy churches are singing churches. Jill Briscoe once told us of a church she had recently visited in the Far East where the believers whisper their singing together because of the dangerous context in which they live, but they still sing because of how indispensable it is to their faith and community. In which direction will your singing this Sunday move your church?

O CHURCH ARISE

In 2005, inspired by Ephesians 6:10–20 and Martin Luther, Keith and Stuart Townend wrote the hymn "O Church Arise":

So Spirit come, put strength in every stride
Give grace for every hurdle
That we may run with faith to win the prize
Of a servant good and faithful
As saints of old still line the way
Retelling triumph of His grace
We hear their calls and hunger for the day
When with Christ we stand in glory.[22]

Luther once said of music, "Music is a gift and grace of God, not an invention of men. Thus it drives out the devil and makes people cheerful. . . . The devil, the originator of sorrowful anxieties and restless troubles, flees before the sound of music almost as much as before the Word of God."[23] Singing God's Word helps us put on our spiritual armor. It helps tighten the belt of truth firmly around our waist and the breastplate of righteousness on our chest; it readies our feet to bring the gospel of peace, strengthens our muscles to hold the shield of faith and the sword of the Spirit in our hands, and steadies the helmet of salvation upon our head.

Our churches are called to "be strong in the Lord and in his mighty power" (Eph. 6:10). We are not a people scurrying into a corner nursing wounds of defeat. We are a city on a hill, stars shining in a dark world, a people of victory and joy, filled with the powerful presence of the Holy Spirit, serving a Savior who shall reign forever. When we sing, it is a battle cry of hope for the wounded, for the weary, for the lost. Sing of Jesus. Sing of your Lord and Savior and greatest Friend. Sing yourself strong. Sing the Church strong. Show up and sing up.

DISCUSSION QUESTIONS

1. How can we serve one another in church with regards to our preferences in congregational singing?

2 How do you prepare for church on a Sunday morning prior to the service? On Saturday night? Throughout the week?

3. What are ways you might respond when your church sings a song in a style you don't particularly enjoy or find engaging?

4. What are the ways your church encourages the music as a communal experience? Are there ways you can support, encourage, and model singing in church as a God-focused communal action?

5. Martin Luther's vision for church singing was one of encouraging Christians as they fought spiritual battles. How much of our church singing today equips us for spiritual battle?

CHAPTER 7

THE RADICAL WITNESS WHEN CONGREGATIONS . . . SING!

*Sing the glory of his name; make his
praise glorious. (Ps. 66:2)*

*Glorious worship is exuberant, never half-hearted.
It is attractive, not off-putting. It is awesome,
never sentimental. It is brilliant not careless. It
points to God, not to the speakers. . . . There is
nothing more evangelistic, nothing that will win
the world more than glorious worship. (*The Songs
of Jesus, *Tim Keller, May 22 Psalm devotion)*

In 1925, just a year after winning an Olympic gold medal in the 400 meter race, the Scottish hero, Eric Liddell, shocked many by deciding to return to China, the place of his birth, as a missionary.

As he stood on the platform of Waverly Station in Edinburgh, crowds gathered to send him off. He was asked to give a few words. Instead, he chose to lead the crowd in a rendition of an old Isaac Watts hymn to communicate more memorably the reason he was leaving fame and ease to preach Christ in a distant land, and to fill his own heart with comfort and confidence:

> *Jesus shall reign where'er the sun*
> *Does its successive journeys run*
> *His kingdom stretch from shore to shore,*
> *Till moons shall wax and wane no more.*

We all sing of a hope that is for all people; a hope we must share. On the wall of a studio in the Moody Radio Headquarters there is a sign that reads, "Your song may be used to save a soul. Sing it prayerfully." We remember reading it again and again as we performed songs for a 9/11 memorial radio program several years ago. But those lines are not true only for a soloist or on a special occasion. They are true for all our singing.

SINGING TOGETHER IS ALWAYS A WITNESS

Our churches are not just places where we are equipped and exhorted to witness to our neighbors who don't know Christ. Our churches are places that themselves bear witness. As the British evangelist Rico Tice puts it:

> It's not only the individual Christian believer who is to let their light shine, a narrow beam of torchlight in the word; each local church is to be a lighthouse: a great, wide beam of gospel light, illuminating the surrounding darkness.[24]

When we sing, we witness to the people in our church who are yet to believe—to the unsaved spouse, the cynical teen, the intrigued friend. We witness to the outsider stepping through the door of a church and even, through the sound we make, to the outsider walking past the door of a church. The sight and sound of a congregation singing praise to God together is a radical witness in a culture that rejects God and embraces individualism. Our songs are the public manifesto of what we believe.

In Matthew 18:20, Jesus says, "For where two or three gather in my name, there am I with them." The numbers He uses are no accident. In Old Testament Israel, you would need "two or three witnesses" in a court to testify on your behalf in a legal case (Deut. 19:15). Singing together bears compelling witness to the truth. It says to those watching on and listening in that, just as we sing the same melody together, we share the same faith, *the* Faith; not a self-made creed for a solo journey toward nowhere, but commitment to our one Lord of all, who transforms the life we live together and will bring us home to eternity.

We witness, too, in the effort we put into our singing. Many churches we have visited schedule times to practice their singing and learn new songs. People generally have ears to hear something that has been done well, and it helps soften a person's heart to the truth.

An old African American spiritual includes this wonderful verse:

If you can't preach like Peter,
If you can't pray like Paul,
You can tell the love of Jesus,
And say "He died for all."
("There Is a Balm in Gilead")

You can *sing* it, too. You can sing of the only hope for this world, and show in the way you sing that you know it is the only hope for this world. Your singing is always a witness. The question is: Is it a good witness or not?

POWERFUL WITNESS

God's people have always witnessed to the truth through their singing. In the Old Testament, the faith of the Israelites could be clearly heard in their songs. And many of the lyrics of their hymnal, the Psalms, showed their awareness of other nations listening into their singing, and called them to praise God too. Psalm 117 says:

> Praise the LORD, all you nations;
> extol him, all you peoples.

> For great is his love toward us,
>> and the faithfulness of the LORD endures forever.
> Praise the LORD.

Given this heritage, it should be no surprise to discover the first New Testament church doing the same:

> Every day they continued to meet together in the temple courts. They broke bread in their homes and ate together with glad and sincere hearts, praising God and enjoying the favor of all the people. And the Lord added to their number daily those who were being saved. (Acts 2:46–47)

The congregational worship in their prayer, their praise, and their actions was a dynamic witness. As Paul put it to the church in Colossae, a church should always be "wise in the way [we] act toward outsiders" so that we can "make the most of every opportunity" (Col. 4:5). "Every opportunity" includes every time a congregation stands up to sing.

Since the dawn of the church, times of great church renewal and revival have been accompanied by (and, we might say, spurred on by) churches singing. As we've already seen, Luther and the Reformers inspired and enabled their congregations to sing together in their own language, in words that they and the people around them could understand. It was revolutionary.

Throughout the history of the British and American revivalist movements (for example those of John and Charles Wesley,

D. L. Moody, and Ira Sankey), congregational singing has been a hallmark and a powerful testimony. Consider the Billy Graham Crusades. Although they were frequently criticized for it, Dr. Graham and his partners included congregational singing at each event so that everyone who gathered could sing the Christian message for themselves and not just hear it. Cliff Barrows, the music director, said, "The Christian faith is a singing faith, and a good way to express it and share it with others is in community singing." There is something unique about congregational singing that is both invitational and instructive to people.

We see it still today each Christmas time. Many people who are yet to believe will visit our churches this December and join with us in singing some of the best and truest poetry ever written. And many of us will take those carols out into our communities to communicate the gospel in schools, malls, hospitals, and countless other local festivals.

SINGING THE GOSPEL

"In Christ Alone" was Keith's first hymn to be released, way back in 2001, cowritten with Stuart Townend. It grew first out of an excitement to write hymns that would help twenty-first-century Christians sing, know, and embrace the incredible truths of the Lord in fresh language, and second out of a frustration with the lack of depth in the songs that were being sung in many churches (in this sense, it was a kind of "protest" music). We envisaged a hymn that told the whole incredible story of the gospel, and settled on the title "In Christ Alone." Keith wrote most of the music, and Stuart wrote most of the (genius) lyrics.

Neither of us ever, ever expected it would be received by the church as it was, and is. Neither of us dreamed we would begin to hear how it was being used as an evangelistic song, explaining the gospel at events where many unbelievers would be attending, including weddings, funerals, and dedications.

We have received countless letters and emails from soldiers on the field, from students in secular universities, from missionaries far from family, and from parents singing at the bedside of a terminally ill child as medical staff listened in, telling how the message of Christ has been proclaimed through that hymn. Just this past week someone told us how one of their friends had been converted halfway through singing it as a teenager on summer camp.

The point is this: being vague and gospel-lite in congregational songs is not the way to be "seeker friendly." Communicating the gospel in a way that informs the mind and engages the emotions is. The gospel is the church's central lyrical distinctive. We should not be shy about it. As you stand and sing in your church this Sunday, you do not know who is listening, and you can never imagine what the Lord might be doing.

A DAMAGING WITNESS

Our girls like to sing a song about cleaning up when we ask them to tidy away their toys or crafts. Often it seems to help with the actual process of tidying up. But it does happen, now and then, that one of them will sing along contentedly without lifting a finger to help—as though singing the song, rather than doing the tidying, is what counts. Neither of us is willing to admit that it's our genes that are to blame . . .

There's the same danger in what we sing in church. We must actually believe and live the truths we sing, otherwise what we sing can make us hypocritical, and not only doesn't attract non-believers—it turns them off. It is easy to sing about the Lordship of Christ; far harder to live under it.

In Deuteronomy, God told Moses something remarkable:

"Write down this song and teach it to the Israelites and have them sing it, *so that it may be a witness for me against them*" (31:19, our italics). Some of Jesus' fiercest words were reserved for religious people who, "honor me with their lips, but their hearts are far from me. They worship me in vain . . ." (Mark 7:6–7). Be careful that what you sing does not expose hypocrisy, and if and where it does, repent and seek God's help to change, and sing the great gospel truths of forgiveness and renewal with all the more feeling in your heart.

Hypocritical living damages our witness and so does half-hearted singing. We remember an uncomfortable conversation with a friend who is not yet a believer. She had listened in to a congregation singing in a service, and having seen how the songs were sung, she questioned if the people there really took seriously what they believed. She said that she had asked herself the same thing many times before in other churches she had visited. Tragically, the way she had seen Christians sing had suggested to her that what they were singing was either not true, or not wonderful, or both. If she were standing near you next Sunday morning, what would she think of your witness?

FACING A TASK UNFINISHED

The hymns we sing together do not only help us in mission, they also call us to mission and sustain us on the mission field, whether that is staying where you grew up or thousands of miles away. In his book *Radical*, David Platt writes, "I could not help but think that somewhere along the way we had missed what was radical about our faith and replaced it with what is comfortable."[25] The words we sing should include thoughts that stir us to action and challenge us with the call of Christ in our lives.

Frank Houghton, once bishop of the East Szechuan area in China and director of China Inland Mission (now OMF), understood how a hymn could motivate people toward compassion for the lost and impel their hearts to go. Following a very raw season of persecution for believers in China, he wrote a missional hymn in the 1930s called "Facing a Task Unfinished." It was first sung at a mission prayer meeting—and it inspired over two hundred missionaries to go and face that task in China. The labors of those missionaries, along with many others, helped grow what was less than a million believers in China to what OMF now estimates to be well over one hundred million. It is thrilling that this very same hymn (with the new "We Go to All the World" chorus) is now being sung by Chinese believers who are passionate about sharing their faith with the children and grandchildren of the believers in the West who once so sacrificially shared it with them.[26]

Our singing is not just a gathering for our own family. The doors are open, there is plenty more room at the table, and there is more than enough food for everyone who is hungry. "God blesses His people with extravagant grace so they might extend his extravagant glory to all peoples on the earth,"[27] David Platt writes. Your singing on Sunday will bear witness to the Savior of the world and fuel your witness through the week to the Savior of the world. And if this chapter has not convinced you to sing the gospel as part of the way you share the gospel, then the words of Frank Houghton's hymn surely will:

> *Facing a task unfinished*
> *That drives us to our knees*
> *A need that, undiminished*
> *Rebukes our slothful ease*
> *We, who rejoice to know Thee*
> *Renew before Thy throne*
> *The solemn pledge we owe Thee*
> *To go and make Thee known*

Where other lords beside Thee
Hold their unhindered sway
Where forces that defied Thee
Defy Thee still today
With none to heed their crying
For life, and love, and light
Unnumbered souls are dying
And pass into the night

We go to all the world
With Kingdom hope unfurled
No other name has power to save
But Jesus Christ the Lord

We bear the torch that flaming
Fell from the hands of those
Who gave their lives proclaiming
That Jesus died and rose
Ours is the same commission
The same glad message ours
Fired by the same ambition
To Thee we yield our powers

O Father who sustained them
O Spirit who inspired
Savior, whose love constrained them

To toil with zeal untired
From cowardice defend us
From lethargy awake!
Forth on Thine errands send us
To labor for Thy sake
(Frank Houghton, "Facing a Task Unfinished," 1931)

DISCUSSION QUESTIONS

1. If I were a visitor to your church and knew nothing of the gospel, what would your church music (selections, presentation, and congregational engagement) convey to me about your faith and understanding of the gospel?

2. How does your church's music connect to the youth and children in your midst?

3. In light of Paul's exhortation to the early church to be mindful that unbelievers are watching as we worship, are you willing to give up your personal preferences so that the singing in your church is a witness to unbelievers?

4. Do we fill our lives with songs that encourage us with cause of mission and the Great Commission? For example, when we read the text to "Facing a Task Unfinished," how might that shape our priorities and passions?

WILL YOU SING?

Evan Roberts was one of the Welsh Revival preachers at the beginning of the twentieth century. He believed in the great importance of singing in spiritual awakening, and in the Christian life. When a Londoner once asked him if he thought the Revival could ever reach the British capital, Roberts is said to have smiled and asked, "Can you sing?"

We love that question. But it's a question that is so easily and damagingly misunderstood. It is not asking, "Can you hold a tune?" "Do you understand harmonies?" "Do you sound good?"

Roberts didn't mean that. What he meant in asking that question was:

"Will you sing?"

And we want to ask you the same question. Will you sing?

This is the most exciting time to be a Christian. The late John Stott had a compelling and urgent vision for the twenty-first-century Church. He inspired multiple generations of believers by helping us to see that this is the most exciting time to be a Christian. There are more Christians in the world than there have ever been before. The Bible can be read in more languages than ever before. The Internet revolution means churches are more connected than ever before, and that mission fields are closer to our reach than ever before.

But this is also a very challenging time to be a Christian. In the West, there is greater opposition to Christian ethics and to the gospel that underpins those ethics than there has been for centuries. There are more dwindling and dying churches than there have been for centuries. The Internet revolution means that Christians are more exposed to heresy than ever before, and that temptations are closer to our reach than ever before.

To borrow from Charles Dickens, this is the best of times, and it is the worst of times. And so the need for believers to hold tightly and loyally to the true Christian faith and to share it with conviction, courage, and compassion has never been more critical.

That means it is vital that we sing together. The songs we sing together are lifelines that draw each of us back to the heart of the King we serve and to the priorities of the kingdom we are members of. The songs we sing to ourselves are what tether us to our Lord day by day. The songs we sing to others are what proclaim His kingdom manifesto in a way that reaches deep into their heads and their hearts.

This book that you have read (unless you skipped straight to the Postlude!) has a very simple aim: that you would sing truth, and sing it as though it is true. As you wake each day, and as you walk through your day, we pray that the lyrics and melodies of your faith will ring around the spaces where you live your life. As you walk into church next Sunday, we pray that you will be excited about sharing in the privilege of lifting your voice with God's people, to "sing and make music from your heart to the Lord." And as you sing, we pray that you would experience the awesome joy of knowing that you are joining in with the great song of praise that resounds through every age, that stretches throughout this world and into every inch of creation, and that is being sung, right now as you read, in the very courts of heaven.

Will *you* sing?

Come, people of the Risen King,
Who delight to bring Him praise;
Come all and tune your hearts to sing
To the Morning Star of grace.
From the shifting shadows of the earth
We will lift our eyes to Him,
Where steady arms of mercy reach
To gather children in.

Come, those whose joy is morning sun,
And those weeping through the night;
Come, those who tell of battles won,
And those struggling in the fight.

For His perfect love will never change,
And His mercies never cease,
But follow us through all our days
With the certain hope of peace.

Come, young and old from every land—
Men and women of the faith;
Come, those with full or empty hands—
Find the riches of His grace.
Over all the world, His people sing—
Shore to shore we hear them call
The Truth that cries through every age:
"Our God is all in all."

Rejoice, Rejoice! Let every tongue rejoice!
One heart, one voice; O Church of Christ, rejoice![28]

Will you *sing*?

DISCUSSION QUESTIONS

1. How has your understanding of the role of music in Christian
   worship changed after reading (and discussing) this book as
   to why we sing, our personal depth and Christian holiness,
   our family life, our commitment to Sunday and the church,
   and our passion for mission?

2. What changes will you make personally to be more engaged in singing the faith?

3. What changes might you suggest for your church to be more engaged as a God-focused, gospel-centered singing community of faith?

BONUS TRACKS

At some point in the near future we look forward to writing a fuller book that focuses more on church musical leadership in all its different areas. But for now, we thought it would be helpful to highlight several of the key issues to kick-start how you might apply the principles outlined in this book. These four extra chapters provide some practical ideas if you have a specific role in encouraging and enabling congregational singing—if you're a pastor, a worship/ song leader, or if you're involved as a musician or on the production team, or as a songwriter.

We are Irish musicians and songwriters, classically educated, emotional firstborns (which explains a lot about us) in our thirties (well, being brutally honest, Keith is in his forties), living in America, raising three daughters, and from a broadly conservative church background. So what comes out in the musical wash is a mixture of all of this. Your context may look very different. So these next pages do not carry exhaustive lists and also need to be carefully applied to your own local church setting.

Even if it is not your area, we have always found it useful to consider all the different roles that support our church's singing. We might then have more compassion and understanding of each other's efforts, and we would likely pray more for those who serve us as we sing.

We know many readers will likely skip the whole book and get to these chapters, the one that is your area or that you're most interested in (that's what we often do with books). But we would recommend a quick glance of at least chapters 2 to 4, and chapter 7, to give a better framing to these more blog-like "bonus tracks."

FOR PASTORS AND ELDERS

We owe an incalculable debt of gratitude to Gilbert Lennox, Bob Lockhart, Alan Wilson, Alistair Begg, and Jim Thomas (and their wives), who have been our pastors from childhood onwards in the five different cities where we have lived. They have taught us, inspired us, held us accountable, prayed for us, championed our work, and given us the benefit of the doubt on more occasions than we deserve. If you are reading this chapter and you are not a pastor, it's important to remember that there is no place in authentic Christian ministry for anyone who does not seek to honor, serve, love, and pray for their leaders (as tricky as that can be for all of us creative personalities).

The one thing we have learned above all others as we have traveled with our music these last ten years is this: Good congregational singing begins with the pastoral leadership.

Whatever the denomination, musical style, or cultural background, the singing is directly proportional to the senior pastor's or leadership team's care for the subject. It is not primarily the music, or the musical leadership, or the budget. Just like parents can't blame their child's ballet teacher if she behaves badly through the week, so the leader of the church, and not the music leader or team, is ultimately responsible for how well the congregation is singing.

Here is a ten-point checklist we suggest for every pastor:

1. Does my congregation know why they sing?

Since congregational singing is something we are created to do by God, commanded to do in God's Word, and compelled to do by the gospel of God, then you need to teach about it. It is ultimately your responsibility to see that this aspect of our worship is explained, nourished, and celebrated. And as it is an area where there has been such a lack of clarity in the last generation, churches need their pastor to teach clearly and positively about it, as well as explain that singing is not a branding exercise, a warm-up for the "main event" of the sermon, nor a means to creating an emotional sensation. That may be through a sermon series, a study series for groups in the church, or a clearly written summary document that church members read and keep. We recommend all three!

2. *Is our church singing strong songs?*

Ultimately, great songs are sung well. Find, or ensure others are hunting out, infectious and emotional melodies combined artistically, in which the wonders of the Lord are described in sung poetry in a way your church just can't wait to sing. Every time you sing one of those types of songs, your congregation will grow in their joy of and commitment to singing together. Every time you sing a song that isn't strong, your congregation's singing drops and people's enthusiasm is diminished. Teaching new songs is important and they should be taught well; but, repeating good songs people have loved and known for a long period of time really encourages confidence.

If you're serving a smaller church that struggles in its singing, we suggest simplicity and depth by building a small canon of Word-filled songs that your church sings really well and then growing slowly from there. Better to know fewer songs and sing them well, than to sing a wide breadth of songs weakly.

3. *Am I part of the weekly song selection process?*

Whether you choose the songs, are actively involved in the process, or simply have clear direction and oversight, it is really important that you know what's going on. After all, the songs are often what your people will go home remembering and repeating (however great your sermon is!). Music may not be an area of expertise for you, but love your congregation enough to care what they are singing.

4. Am I overseeing the overall selection or "canon" of songs?

In the online generation, it is possible for us to write a song, put it online, and then have it used in six continents that weekend. While this has strengths, it means the pool of songs is often larger than previous generations, and that there is less accountability over their creation and an inbuilt tendency to favor what's new simply because it's new.

This also means that, if songs are chosen one by one and simply on their own merits, churches can end up with a narrow range of songs in terms of their depth and breadth theologically. Ensure that your church's song list includes hymns and songs that touch on all the major doctrines and seasons of life, just as the Psalms and historical hymnals do.

5. Am I passionately involved in the singing?

The great Welsh preacher of the last century, Martyn Lloyd-Jones, insisted on personally leading the pastoral prayer week to week because he took modeling prayer to his congregation so seriously. We'd argue that this sort of care should be given to the singing as well, not necessarily with a microphone on, or even at the front, but singing visibly before the congregation.

A pastor who seems distracted or half-hearted, or who indeed is often not even in the room, is telling his congregation that singing is not that important to him. Sing to your people. Be present, be engaged, and be passionate. If you are not, then they will not be either.

6. *Am I leading, encouraging, teaching, and building strong relationships with all the musicians?*

When a pastor pours into his lead musicians, they become more informed, more in step with the vision and mission of the church, and often much more creative and energized in what they do. Encouragement is oxygen to the creative soul.

A church music department left unchecked can become like a monster in a church, wielding too much influence and causing a lot of grief. It is not healthy for the whole congregation or for the musicians themselves if the relationship between the pastor(s) and them is not operating well.

In church leadership it is always tempting to avoid hard conversations, and there is oftentimes no one more difficult for a pastor than lead musicians, who tend to be popular, strong, and emotional. But those conversations need to happen or everybody suffers. When music directors and their pastors form deep, committed, trusting, robust, and mutually respectful working partnerships, the opportunity for ministry is incalculable.

7. Do I regularly encourage the congregation in their singing?

Give your congregation encouragement. Week by week, help grow the congregation's confidence, and listen out for their voices. If you are leading the service, give short reflections on aspects of what has been or is about to be sung, and encourage your flock to sing to one another as an expression of their gospel unity. Tell the stories of the songs you are singing from time to time. And encourage the church's gratitude for and support of the music team.

8. Am I encouraging the congregation to prepare for Sunday services?

Encourage individuals to be praying about what they will do on Sunday; encourage families to have bulletins or hymnbooks or some resource that teaches them the gospel in their home life; and encourage them to sing together (see chapter 6). Promote listening to songs on smartphones and at home in everyday life. Email song lists, send links to YouTube videos and sheet music, and so on.

9. Am I planning the service order in a sensitive and creative way?

In all art, the order and timing of everything can enhance the meaning and beauty of the experience, or it can obscure it—and a church service is no different.

The overall arc of a service should help shape our understanding of the gospel—the greatness of God, the wonder of forgiveness in Christ through the repentance of our sin, and our prayers for the growth of Christ's kingdom in our lives and the world.

The beginning of the service should help establish the singing. Pentecostal traditions often sing continuously for forty minutes or more at the start of a service—while that may be a culture shock for your church, the principle of starting with familiar songs, or even doing pre-service singing, is well worth considering. We also recommend using your song choices to enhance the message of the passage and the focus of the preached message, especially in terms of singing in response at the end of the service.

10. Am I overseeing the development of singing in congregational life?

Part of the vision for your church should include how you would love to see the singing develop. Keep the leadership team accountable to these goals. If you show intentionality and care about the singing in your church, sooner or later everyone else will (and vice versa).

This might also mean figuring out when the whole church can sing together, all age groups. For example, both of our home churches (in Belfast and in Nashville) include the children in the first part of the singing in the main worship service.

And finally . . . for one year, make the first question you ask about music at the weekly church review meeting: "How did the congregation sing?"

WORSHIP AND SONG LEADERS

Both the one who makes people holy and those who are made holy are of the same family. So Jesus is not ashamed to call them brothers and sisters. He says, "I will declare your name to my brothers and sisters; in the assembly I will sing your praises." (Heb. 2:11–12)

CHRIST IS OUR WORSHIP LEADER

Before we jump to the checklist in this chapter, we thought it would be good to simply state that Christ is our ultimate worship leader, the Choirmaster of heaven and earth. Both the deep conviction of our hearts and the visible outworking of our gifting should be informed by the knowledge that we all have equal access to Christ, the Mediator of us all (Heb. 4:16; 1 Tim. 2:5; Eph. 3:12).

We must make sure we serve people in their singing in such a way that points the congregation clearly to Christ and not to us, or a mood we are trying to set, as their "mediator." Our songs must be filled with the person and works of Christ, our gestures must defer to Him as Lord, and our arrangements and production help them freely sing to Him in spirit and in truth.

DEFINING THE ROLE

In most churches today, the singing is led broadly in one of three ways:

1. A "worship leader," who has an active role and is usually a lead singer.
2. The service is all led by a pastor, with a lead singer and musicians in assisting roles.
3. As above, but with instrumental or choral-based leadership.

We appreciate there are people reading this book who feel strongly about all three traditions, as well as those with differing nuances (in leadership, musical, singing, and liturgical styles). Regardless of definition, we have addressed these general points to those who are musically leading the singing in church. This is a crucial role as we point a congregation to the glory of God and the story of redemption through our singing together in a way that is beautiful and faith building for all. In every context, it is presumed that the pastoral and music teams work in good creative collaboration. It can't be said often enough that there is no place in musical leadership for those who do not follow the leaders of their church as they seek to serve the members of their church.

1. Am I walking with the Lord?

Your primary relationship is your own relationship with the Lord. "A man is what he is on his knees before God, and nothing more," as the nineteenth-century Scottish pastor, Robert Murray McCheyne, put it. You don't suddenly step into "worshipper clothes" when you walk in front of people. Your passion for leading sung worship in your church will only ever be healthy if your relationship with God is healthy—if you are in the Word, praying regularly, and living as part of your church community and knowing accountability there. Anyone in a leadership role serves as an example to others on and off the platform.

Lead with joy and thankfulness. This does not mean that you must affect a surface of happiness, but rather that there should be a steady beat of joy in your demeanor and expression that inspires the people you lead to sing to the Lord and to each other. Thankfulness to Christ should shape the disposition of your spirit and your talents. It will lift you up in confidence when you feel inadequate, it will soften you from the frost of cynicism, and it will tether you with proper humility when your ego is tempted to swell.

2. Am I in good relationship with my church leader(s)?

You share a platform that is not yours and you serve the leadership and their vision and mission for the church you are in. It is essential to develop a good system of communication, on and off the platform, with those who have been called to pastor your church (which includes you). Where you disagree with the approach of the leaders, continue to serve without gossip or malice. If the conflict is too great to reconcile, move on to somewhere else so that your frustration does not snowball and knock other people down.

Behind everything we do there must be a disposition of the heart that is soft and submissive to the Lord, and to those who are leading us as we lead others. Leading worship is not to master what seems like some sort of magical calling. It is a God-given gifting, to be used to serve His church and glorify His Son.

3. Am I investing in relationships with my music team(s)?

Your team must be in right relationship with God and with each other, and it is your job to lead and seek that. There should be an environment of mutual encouragement, friendship, and enthusiasm for each other's gifts.

Our dealings with one another in private should also be God-honoring, lest, having stood in the open together to sing of our allegiance to Christ, we should privately stumble together—in gossip, in impurity, in divisiveness.

For example, as we travel on the road and in our offices, we have a rule that a man and woman (unless they are married) are not to be alone together in a closed room, an elevator, a car, or another isolated space. This helps keeps us as a team far from any suspicion and above reproach in this area.

4. Am I choosing good songs?

Aim for your choices, like the Psalms, to give:

- A vast vision of God's character
- How we fit into God's redemption story
- A broad understanding of human experience

Consider carefully the lyrics of the songs you gather together for a particular service. Ask:

- Is this true of who Christ is and all He has done and is doing and will do for us, in us, and through us?
- Is this filled with the freedom of the gospel?
- Does it provide language for sincere praise and renewed faith and loyal obedience?
- What image of Christ is it giving to the unbeliever?

As you review the music afterward, ask:

- Did the congregation sing well?
- Was the Word proclaimed?
- Was it honoring to the Lord?

5. Am I committed to serving my congregation?

Your relationship with the congregation is hugely important. It is not just you and the Lord by yourself, in front of an audience whose presence is arbitrary. You are with your family, and they are looking to you to guide them and not merely to perform to them. When asking, "What do I wear?" "What do I do with my hands?" "How will I stand?" "What should I say?" and so on, let the congregation's benefit be your guide. Even as your own heart is focusing on the Lord (and often the many other things that pull for your attention), part of your worship to the Lord is to serve their good.

Be prayerful. Be clear about what you are doing. Every word you speak should thoughtfully serve the purpose of the singing within that particular service—whether it's a verse from Scripture that helps invite people in, or the direction to stand, or a brief prayer of response to close a time of singing.

One concerning observation we have made is that in many churches, both the leadership and the congregation would much prefer a wider range of musical style and expression than the worship leaders are willing or able to give. Take care not to bottleneck the flow of congregational singing by only singing what you like and do best.

6. Am I encouraging the congregational voice?

Help people find their voice. Look for it. In doing so, you will cultivate a culture in which it is strange to be a passive congregant.

One of the things our church (The Village Chapel in Nashville) does increasingly is singing unaccompanied at some point during the service to inspire the congregational voice and to encourage harmonies.

The focus you have on encouraging the congregational voice will lead to certain compromises in your personal preferences. For example, your voice may sound better in one key over another, but if you can sing to a good solid standard in the key that's better for the congregation, you should do that. If you only ever sing the songs that perfectly suit your voice, you are probably not serving the congregation in the best way. A lot of our recordings are in lower keys as it's more comfortable for Kristyn, but when we lead the same song in church we arrange it in a higher key so that it better fits the majority of voices.

Singing to lead in church is not the same as singing to be a soloist. Try to make sure your phrasing and breathing is clear for the benefit of the congregation following on. The beginnings of phrases are usually the most important, so make the first words of the verse and of the chorus strong so the congregation knows where they are (a visible breath from you before helps too). Take liberties with style only where the congregation is confident in singing that song, so that what you are doing adds to, rather than detracts from, their ability to sing and enjoyment of it.

If you are using a new song, teach it. Email the congregation in advance if you can with a link to the lyrics and a video of the song; if you can, set aside the time to practice them together. If you have a choir, one Sunday you could "plant" the choir amongst the congregation to help encourage the singing.

7. Am I being myself rather than trying to be someone else?

Know your strengths and (where possible) fill the gaps so that a broad and diverse congregation can lean and depend on their music leaders. Don't feel that you need to copy someone else's style as it may seem awkward or affected on you. Trust that God has given you just the gifts He knows you need to lead the particular flock of His that you are serving.

Help your musicians to play like themselves and not always to mimic a recording. It would be better for everyone in the room if we played to our own strengths, simplifying where we needed to and adapting an arrangement of a song in such a way that really released the congregation to sing.

8. Am I mindful of the work of the Holy Spirit?

"When the Advocate comes, whom I will send to you from the Father—the Spirit of truth who goes out from the Father—he will testify about me" (John 15:26). Are we singing in a way that is submissive to the Spirit, testifying to Christ?

We are to be "filled with the Spirit" as we sing (Eph. 5:18). Pray that the Holy Spirit might grow the fruits of His presence in the way you fulfill your ministry role. For example, ask Him for a deeper love for your church as you gather together, increasing joy in all your celebration, patience where the singing is not as musical as you would like, forbearance where a style is not your favorite, kindness as you encourage others, goodness as you respect one another in purity through what you wear or how you move, faithfulness to tell the gospel to the next generation, gentleness toward those who are coming to church hurting or confused, and self-control to conduct yourself in a way that honors the Lord, however the service may go and whatever people may say afterward.

There are moments when the person in leadership may change course a little. But the Spirit also works in the preparation and practice we do in advance, for spiritual intuition is not always to be equated with spontaneity.

We have led music in services that had a printed liturgical order of service where all elements were worked out in advance, and we have led worship where we have changed the "script" a little as we go; sometimes we've repeated a chorus or even swapped out a song. We have worked with musicians skilled at improvising and orchestras who expertly follow the sheet music in front of them. Is one way more Spirit-led than the other? No. We do not control Him, nor should we assume we know how He will work every time.

The Holy Spirit is not necessarily pressing in more closely when there is a musical experience created that heightens the senses, whether it be through a musical motif, a change of lights, or a haze in the air. Hold these things with an open hand and exercise caution, as they are sometimes not the best things for congregational singing. In fact, they can be damaging if people determine how "spiritual" a worship service was exclusively by how they *felt* during the singing.

9. Am I growing old gracefully?

When we moved to Nashville, our friend Eric Wyse said to us that it was a rare thing to see a musical professional in this music city grow old gracefully. It is hard to be objective, to see physical strength fade, to not let the privilege of ability and visibility swallow up your sense of identity, to let go when you need to and share the roles, to seek out, train up, and encourage others coming after you—but it is essential for your well-being and for the well-being of the church in which you serve.

Equally and conversely, don't allow youth to be the idol of church music leadership. Our Western culture is different from many other world cultures in prizing youth over honoring age, and that must not seep into our churches. It is helpful and inspiring to see a church music ministry that is multi-generational, each learning and leaning on one another, delighting in the strength different talents and insights bring.

10. Am I walking with the Lord?

This is the first question to ask—and it is the last. Too many of us dry up in faith without anyone noticing because we are up on stage. Better to drop out of leading worship than drop out of your faith. Invest in your relationship with Jesus, for everything else you do must flow from that.

MUSICIANS, CHOIRS, AND PRODUCTION

Praise the LORD with the harp;
make music to him on the ten-stringed lyre.
Sing to him a new song;
play skillfully, and shout for joy. (Ps. 33:2–3)

We learned to sing and play music growing up in our local churches; our faith, the songs we sang, and the ways in which we sang and played them all leaned on each other in a way that was hard to separate. We weren't taught the distinction between performer and worshipper; learning to perform well in a way that encouraged the congregation in their singing was an extension of a life of worship.

Over the years since we first learned, we have been privileged to work with incredible musicians and production techs, many of whom are our closest friends. The artist Sting once said that he always tried to surround himself with musicians who were better than him, so that he would both always be learning, and always sound better—we have found this to be very true.

A NOTE ON CHOIRS

We love choirs!

We like to work with choirs as much as we can. The majority of our concerts over the years have been supported by choirs, and Keith in particular has been in and worked with choirs most of his life.

While we enjoy hearing anthems and special performance music, what we appreciate most (and what we think is the central calling of the church choir) is a choir's ability to help the congregation sing better, as those with strong vocal ability help everyone else sing out familiar tunes and navigate newer ones. If you sing in a choir, you are a musician, serving a congregation with your gifts.

A MUSICIAN'S CHECKLIST

Here are five questions for you to ask yourself if you are a musician, a singer, or a band member. If you're part of the "production team," you'll find a five-point checklist on page 129.

1. How can I best accompany the congregation's singing?

Primarily and fundamentally, you are there to help God's people sing. It is not a restriction or reduction of your talent to do so—you put loving your neighbor as yourself into practice as you help God's family sing. Only fools think their artistry is more important than serving the congregation.

The question to ask yourself and your fellow musicians after a service is: "How did we help the congregation sing?"

2. Am I a team player?

The purpose of your performance is to draw the church together and not widen the divide between the stage and the rest of the room. You are part of "Team Congregation." Play skillfully so that people can shout for joy, but do not show off in any way that makes it harder for people to jump in and sing along. You may need to simplify the lines you play, straighten out the rhythm of a line you are singing, turn the volume down on your amplifier, or take one of your in-ear monitors out so that you can hear the congregation.

Sing to God and to those around you (or, if you're on stage, in front of you). It's important to model wholehearted engagement, so, if and when you can, sing with joy and passion while you play. Aim to make the entries into verses and choruses or a repeated verse/chorus particularly clear, so that the congregation knows where you are in a song. Entries into a song are incredibly important.

You are also part of "Team Musicians." Be united in this effort to encourage and enable corporate praise. Defer gladly to those in leadership and to one another. Accept the role you play in any given song.

On a touring weekend, Keith could accompany "In Christ Alone" on the guitar with our girls at night time, who are learning the words and go at their own speed; then play the same song in a radio station on a keyboard with Kristyn; then play it on a grand piano in a large, formal church; and then play it a fourth time in an arena with the band at a concert. All four contexts are very different and require different listening and different playing. In each, musicians are team members. So are you.

3. Am I practicing and preparing properly?

We must prepare thoroughly to play well for God's people—it should never be done to anything less than our best. When we first moved to Nashville, one of the most surprising experiences for us was hiring an "A-list" musician to play with us at a conference. When he asked for the song list, we apologized for our indecision and emailed two possible lists to him. When we arrived at the event, he was in his seat one hour before rehearsal (and before everyone else), had recharted every song on both lists, having studied the live versions, and had a couple of questions. It was frightening just how thoroughly great musicians prepare. If they who are at the top of their craft work that hard, let's not kid ourselves that we don't need to.

If you commit to playing, commit to loving the people in your church enough to prepare well. A lot of people who play in church have other jobs and so have divided time, but there is a cost to serving—and if you're a musician, part of it is making sure you carve out good space to be ready. Bob Kauflin writes, "The goal of practice isn't doing something until you get it right. It's doing it until you can't get it wrong."[29] If you struggle with nerves, extra preparation may just be the magic bullet that moves you from thinking and worrying about yourself to focusing on and enjoying the congregation as you play.

Make sure, as much as you are able, that you sleep Saturday night, and that you're punctual and organized on Sunday. Be prayerful before you arrive.

4. Do I love my leadership . . . and my church family?

Music groups are notorious for attracting colorful, strong, often socially insensitive or emotionally inconsistent people. (We are allowed to say that because we're musicians!)

Make sure that your aim is to promote unity even at the expense of your personal preferences, not to undermine it in order to secure those preferences. Prayerfully honor both your church leader and music leader, not only by following their lead, but by doing so without grumbling or complaining. Ask them how you can play a better role in helping the congregation sing. And aim as a group of musicians to serve the church beyond your music. Many choirs are a prayer engine in their church and great providers of hospitality. Being on stage should only ever be a small part of your service and certainly never the totality of it.

5. Am I growing my gifting?

Whatever gift you have for accompanying God's people singing, try to improve in your use of it, so that you can better serve your church.

If you're a singer, it could involve being in a choir, theatre company, or taking voice lessons. For musicians, you might record your piano playing and actively listen back to it, take classes, ask advice from musicians you admire, or play in an orchestra. Constantly be listening to great music and surround yourself with people who are life-giving in creativity.

Most of all, grow in your love for Christ. As young musicians, John Lennox challenged us "to grow in your musical gifting but make sure your faith grows even faster." To be a musician in God's service is to be His first, and then to make music to His glory as excellently and beautifully as you can. There are no short-cuts in this and no finish line in learning.

A special word to choirs here—church music styles do change, and you have to be prepared to be flexible to stay involved. It's key to be willing to vary stylistically, allow subgroups to thrive, and share the stage.

FIVE QUESTIONS FOR PRODUCTION TEAMS

Production—whether you are a one-man band or part of a team—is an act of service, and it goes hand in hand with the technical expertise required to facilitate singing. We have worked with some wonderful sound engineers and producers. We have experienced the joys of things working well and the tensions and temptations when technology does not cooperate. We are thankful for the decisions our local church here in Nashville made to use technology and production to support the congregational singing in the best way they could in the main spaces that we meet.

Folks who serve us like this are mostly behind the scenes, and tend to be criticized when technical issues arise but not applauded when things go well. Many are volunteers. If you are reading this and you are not a member of your church's production team, please find them this Sunday and thank them.

Here are a few things that we think members of the production teams whom we have really valued have been asking themselves about their role:

1. Am I favoring the congregation's singing in my balancing of the sound?

People will have differing opinions on the sound in the room—it can be a very subjective thing. But (and particularly given that many of our meeting spaces were unfortunately not designed for group singing) the balance of sound should do what it can to serve the whole church, which means sometimes turning things up and sometimes turning down. Listen to the congregation and not just the stage so you can get the best sound to help the singing.

2. Are the words clear to the congregation?

The job of the person running the screen (or, of course, putting the church hymnal in each seat and the number on the wall or in the bulletin) is so important. If you are in charge of changing the words on the screen(s), anticipate the breath a congregation will make before the first words on the screen, and make sure you are with them. Don't come in mid-word or sentence, as people see a little ahead of the sound they will sing. Present the words in a clear font. Words are regularly accompanied by video, but (though we have seen this done well) please consider whether the congregation would actually sing better without the distraction.

When using a hymnal, make sure people know where to turn to. Clear instructions are particularly helpful to the visitor, or when a song is not well-known.

In all you do, aim to give people confidence to sing by taking away anything that might hinder them.

3. Have I remembered I am not working in a stadium or large theater?

Often people in production (and indeed, in the congregation!) go to a conference and come home frustrated that the sound or lights are not as good in their church. Don't be discouraged. If it's the congregational voice you are encouraging, you really do not need all those other things. For thousands of years people were able to sing without stage lights or a sound desk! Work from where you are and develop slowly, as you are able. Do the best you can with the space and the kit you have.

4. Am I paying attention to detail?

We are so very grateful for the administrative superheroes, those who care for the big and small details so that the team at the front can do their job and the congregation is well-served. Whatever your role, you are serving the Lord by serving His people, so be encouraged in it and do your best with it. Administrative skills are a God-given gift.

5. Is my heart in the right place?

Even if you are not on stage, you can still end up doing your role in order to bring yourself glory (or be annoyed when you get no glory); and you can still end up seeing your part and department as more important than others. Pray about your job beforehand, remember whom it is you are serving, and, just as with pastors and musicians, see your "success criteria" not as whether you got the balance just right or the lighting came up on cue as you'd hoped, but rather: "How did I help the congregation sing?"

SONGWRITERS AND CREATIVES

It is my plan, following the example of the prophets and
ancient fathers of the church, to compose vernacular
psalms for the masses; that is spiritual songs, so that
the Word of God might also remain in song among
the people. To this end we are searching everywhere
for poets. (Martin Luther, Worship Wars in Early
Lutheranism, *chapter 1, Letter to Georg Spalatin, 1523)*

In recent years, songwriting for congregational singing seems to have become a more and more interesting topic for people, and so we wanted to include something on it in this book. But when it comes to songwriting, the two of us are students, not masters. We are always learning how to do it, and we find it so difficult. We work long hours for small results. We wish it was faster. We wish it was easier. For others, it comes quicker and more painlessly, but for us it is an exciting, heartfelt, privileged, desperately frustrating process that often feels like pulling teeth. So our thoughts here are more about what we aim for and pray for in our writing, rather than about what we always achieve in it!

1. When writing for the church, write for your church.

Your only focus should be writing for your church, not trying to give oxygen to other personal musical ambitions or agendas. The nonnegotiables in anything you write is that it has biblical integrity, and is inspiring and memorable to sing musically.

When writing for the church, you are writing with a very specific goal. Lots of people need to be able to sing the lyrics. They need to capture the heart of our faith, our imaginations, and our experience of life, within a community setting.

So ask: What are the lyrics your church needs to sing? What is the melody they will be able to sing?

Always compose hearing the congregational voice in your mind, rather than your favorite artist, or someone on the radio, or something your learned in your classical music training.

It is also really helpful if your writing leans into what your church is doing—it makes the songs more relevant and also a more natural fit. It's great to write for special events in your church (e.g., children's summer camp, Christmas musical, a Sunday series on the Psalms).

The more you try to write well into your church context, the more original you will be. The more you try to copy the popular thing of the moment, the less original you will be.

2. Find an appropriate outlet for your work to explore its potential.

You need to try songs out, whether it is among music groups, home groups, youth groups, or groups of friends. If a song "works" in that setting, and there is an excitement from the church leadership, try songs in the church.

Once a song is being requested by your congregation or individual members on a regular basis, then share it with partner churches and friends who would be interested. Do this only when you are sure about the song, as you will build confidence with others only when they really love it. Then see where it goes from there. Very few of the songs we write ever get to this stage, and there are some that got through that we should have worked longer on.

3. Be realistic in your expectations.

To write songs for the church is a beautiful, fun (sometimes), and laudable activity. But most songs that are written (in the case of songs we have written, at least 95 percent) never should be heard. We estimate Keith has written or recorded five hundred to a thousand tunes per year for the last seventeen years, in order to come up with what is a relatively small handful of songs that we're pleased with and known for. Kristyn has countless journals and Word files and scrap pieces of paper with lyrics that never made the cut.

Even after that, some are for ourselves, some for our family and friends, and most of the rest for a limited church community for a limited period of time.

The reality television generation has suggested that unless you gain instant fame and wealth, your music has somehow not reached its potential. This is a breeding ground for bitterness and discontent. So you need to maintain realistic expectations.

4. Be a student of the art form.

Songwriting is an art form and not theological propaganda, so study art and beauty. Keith practiced, studied, or rehearsed music five to eight hours per day for ten years and wrote melodies for four years before the first album was released.

Study melodies that work well for the congregation and ask why they work. Dissect them and consider the techniques and forms. We once had the pleasure of having dinner with the great choral composer John Rutter and asked him about his writing process. He simply answered, "It is technique." It was a craft he worked at like a potter with clay.

It's the same with lyrics. You cannot pull water out of a dry well. When writing for the church, the main water source is the living Word of God. Drink it in as much as you can, without abdicating any responsibilities of parenting and so on that the Lord has given you. Fill your imagination with all types of good literature. Kristyn studied English Literature at university and not classical music. Have a plan and find accountability to help you walk through that plan. If you are a songwriter for the church, you bear part of the responsibility for the canon of songs your church sings. It is your responsibility to make sure the lyrics are as excellent and true and life-giving as you can possibly make them. A good melody with unhelpful words is a powerful and deadly combination. A good lyric can be lost and unsung if the melody is not good enough, but the opposite is not true—a good melody will be sung even if the lyric is not great.

5. *Crave fresh language and sound.*

Speaking of lyrics, there is always something more to write. By definition, the created never can grasp the whole mind of its Creator. There is always another angle, another emphasis, a different voicing.

So "Jesus Loves Me" is just as valid, just as loved, just as important a song as "O the Deep Deep Love of Jesus." Both have a similar theme, both have devotional elements but to different effect; one is helpful in its simplicity, and the other is helpful in its greater complexity. Both are profound. Both are honoring to God. But we don't sing songs like "Jesus Loves Me" all the time and we don't sing songs like "O the Deep Deep Love of Jesus" all the time.

The Psalms are actually fresher and more interesting than a lot of our songlists. They both narrow and widen the scope of every theme they expound. Ninety percent of Christian songs are about 10 percent of the themes in the Psalms. Explore new themes and write new melodies. Always have a thirst to find new and fresh sounds. Seek out music that is not as familiar to you. If we pursue only what sounds current in our culture in our moment, then we are guaranteeing that before long our music will sound dated.

6. Grow lyrics like trees grow.

A good hymn is an organic whole where all the parts connect to one another in a thoughtful, coherent, and poetic way. When approaching a hymn lyric, we have found it helpful to imagine the hymn as a tree.

We begin with the seed of an idea—what is the song about, where would it be used in a service, if it were in a hymnal where would it be placed on the category page. Maybe it's a song for communion, or about creation, or the mystery of God.

Once that seed is planted in our imagination, we begin to grow the trunk and branches—the structure of the song. What is the thought flow, and what are the important ideas (knowing that a song can't carry everything you would ever want to say)? How will each verse develop the theme? If there is a chorus, what is the key thought that is worthy of repetition and that drives home the message of the song?

After this is in place, we grow the leaves—we shape the language and form the poetry. First lines are particularly important as they draw people in and help unlock the whole song. Last lines are also important, driving people toward a big vision or challenge of commitment or expression of praise. We are looking for delightful phrases, little twists on things we have heard before, both freshness and familiarity, easily understood but engaging. It is a challenge!

(Sometimes you may have had a first thought of a "leaf" or word or phrase before you ever thought of the "seed," and so you work backward to the seed, because you still need to see the vision for the whole piece.)

One of the challenges in songwriting is aiming to inspire response through revelation and not tell or describe to people how to feel. Just as a joke only works if you don't have to tell a listener that it's funny, so it's much more effective to fill your verses and choruses about God than to tell people how to feel about Him. This is something we are always having to learn and haven't always done well. It is easy to be sentimental or manipulative when you write. But it is always best not to be.

7. *Work collaboratively.*

We have worked mostly in collaboration when we write, and that has created useful artistic tension as we each come from different angles. It helps give a breadth of musical skill, and it also provides a sense of community and support. It often makes songwriting more fun, and even more often makes it humbling. It builds good feedback into the process, throughout the process. It is not always a pleasant part of songwriting, but many good songs would never be what they are without it.

8. Editing is your friend.

Every good writer knows the value of a good editor.

We have had moments—very rare moments!—where a lyric has come very easily.

More often, we need to go over a line again and again, cutting things, adding things, even changing structural things around. But sooner or later a song that is to be sung must come into the light, so find encouraging but wise and sensible friends who can see things more clearly than you can when you have been poring over your work closely.

Alistair Begg talks about how the measure of a well-made suit is the material that is left on the ground. Often it is the things we take out that allow a song to breathe and have a much more powerful and beautiful impact. The leftovers may even make another song, one day.

9. Lean in to your unique creative DNA and background.

Keith grew up in a home where music was discussed and enjoyed in wide varieties of contexts—his mum taught piano in the house while his dad was often preparing for choir practice, playing the organ, or singing in a local choir, which constantly stretched his musical tastes. While the central theme in the music in his house was church music, it was as likely to be Haydn's "Creation" as hymns and beautiful liturgical music from Kings College Cambridge. He was in a Bible study group of teenage boys who knew more about the Puritan writings of John Owen than Jon Bon Jovi in this remote part of Northern Ireland, and long hours were spent trying to play melodies on a flute and find new chords on a piano or guitar and studying historical high-church music both at The Friends School and at Durham University.

Kristyn, a pastor's kid, grew up in the rich bustle of local church life, learning music by ear, involved in the contemporary/traditional blend of the adult and children's music ministry teams. She was regularly surrounded by great conversation around the dinner table with her parents and the many theologians, missionaries, and church leaders they invited in, as well as nurtured in a love for literature through the influence of her dad and English literature teachers at Ballyclare High School and Queen's University.

The unique blend of all of this was the foundation on which the hymns we write were built. Your blend will be different. Your background and your natural tastes and your creative abilities are not the same as ours. That's a good thing! Be yourself as you write.

10. Four questions for arranging songs for congregations to sing:

- What sets up the song for the congregation to sing best?

- What is the essence of the song, and how can I make this arrangement allow the music to express that?
- How can I write to the strengths of my players? What bearing do player combinations, personnel, and rehearsal time available have on the arrangement?
- Is there a context linked to the song, service, or musicians that would allow something fresh? (This should not be forced . . . the answer may well be "no.")

A FINAL CODA

Gary Haugen, CEO of the International Justice Mission, recently shared with us a story about a civil rights leader who, early in the struggle, was resoundingly defeated and came home an apparent failure. When asked if he was encouraged by anything in the whole episode, he said that he had been hugely encouraged, because in the midst of his defeat he had become finally convinced they would one day win. Why? Because they had the songs the people were singing . . . the melodies that would carry the movement. He knew that whoever has the songs has the people.

John Newton, in the preface of one of his hymn collections published in 1779, wrote of those he was writing songs for that "while my hand can write, and my tongue speak, it will be the business and pleasure of my life, to aim at promoting their growth and establishment in the grace of our God and Savior." Let that be your aim too, in all the writing and arranging that you do.

ACKNOWLEDGMENTS

The first day we met was in May 1999, and we wrote a song together. We have worked together ever since, getting married along the way and having three lovely daughters.

We thought we had learned most of what needed learning about writing with your spouse, but then we turned from songwriting for a while and started on a book together. Keith described it as "giving birth" (little do men know—he only suggested that once).

We have certainly never felt a greater debt of gratitude to the encouragement and wisdom of those God has put in our lives to help us craft the message of this book, suffer our borderline neurosis, and cheer us on as individuals, as a married couple, as parents, as musicians, as local church members, and as fellow singers of the gospel.

Thank you to our daughters—Eliza, Charlotte, and Grace—for teaching us so much about singing together as a family and for being with us on all our adventures. What a joy it is to be your parents.

Thank you to our parents—John, Helen, Gilbert, and Heather—for introducing us to love, life, Christ, and singing His praise, and to siblings and family who had their childhoods constantly interrupted and frustrated by our energy and noise.

We are hugely indebted to the constant kindness and support of our pastors and local churches—Glenabbey Church in Belfast, Northern Ireland (Gilbert Lennox, David Mairs, Chris Cooke); to Alistair and Sue Begg at Parkside Church, who brought us to the USA, advised us throughout the whole project (including warning us not to write a book until Keith turned forty), and continues to be a supporting church at large; and then to Jim and Kim Thomas at The Village Chapel here in Nashville, Tennessee, who have provided a spiritual home, pastoral support, an unparalleled creative community, and a beautiful singing congregation to remind us every week of the joy it is to sing to the Lord.

Thank you to all at LifeWay and B&H—particularly Dr. Thom Rainer for his vision, Mike Harland for all our breakfasts, and Jennifer Lyell and Devin Maddox, who are probably shaking their heads in disbelief that this project finally met a finishing line. Thank you for the freedom and grace you gave us and the excitement you had for this from before day one. Thank you to Robert Wolgemuth (and Nancy) and his team who walked us through the factory of book making and always had enthusiasm for what we were trying to do.

Thank you to the music and literature teachers and creative collaborators we have been privileged to study under and to work with—too many to possibly mention, except of course the genius of Stuart Townend that has helped shape, sharpen, contradict, and articulate so many of our ideas.

Thank you to our Getty Music Team—Greg McNey, Joni McCabe, Josh Sutton, Beverly Bartsch, Becky Haight, and Peter Wahlers. Thank you to Brettan Cox and Abby Wahlers, who came alongside us to help care for our children through these last months. Thank you to our band who have traveled many miles with us to accompany congregational singing.

Thank you to those key people who also spoke very deeply into our lives and work, especially as we processed this book over many phone calls and emails and a lot of coffee (Keith) and chocolate (Kristyn). We particularly want to thank Carl Laferton for helping us shape this book, Don Carson, Tim Keller, Paul Tripp, Joni Eareckson Tada, David Platt, Lawrence Kimbrall, Matt Merker, Jonathan Rea, Alistair Begg, Jim and Kim Thomas, Trevin Wax, Tim Challies, Robert Morgan, Paul McNulty, Sam Logan and all at WRF, Stephen Cave, John Martin, Ed Stetzer, Warren Smith, Stephen Nichols, Gary Millar, Rick Holland, Bob Lepine, Os Guinness, Jon Duncan, Joe Crider, Tommy Bailey, Steve Guthrie, Deborah Klemme, and Eric Wyse.

Thank you to Dave and June Bullock, true "psalm singers"—those who have testified to God's faithfulness in song and in life through every season, especially in these last years through the loss of their son. You are among our longest friends in America, and we are so grateful to you in more ways than you could ever know.

Thank you to the many churches and groups who have hosted us over this last decade of touring; the old and new friends and places that helped grow and focus our understanding and passion for congregational singing.

Thank you, reader and fellow singer, for the opportunity this book affords to hopefully help inspire you and your congregation or music leadership with a vision for congregational singing. We stand on the tall shoulders of those who went before us, who in writing songs and thinking thoughts gave us the rich heritage we all have in the hymnody and musical expression of the Church today. May these musings join the effort to elevate the attention given to singing in the life of the local church and also in the days to come until the Lord returns. For then our voices will join the angels and all the saints who have gone before us and have come after us to fill the courts of heaven in praise to the One who sits on the throne. All praise and thanks and honor and power be to Him for ever and ever, Amen.

Keith and Kristyn, Nashville, Tennessee

NOTES

1. Attributed to Martin Luther in *Devotional Warm-Ups for the Church Choir: Preparing to Lead Others in Worship* by Kenneth W. Osbeck (Grand Rapids, MI: Kregel Publications, 2000).

2. Os Guinness, *Fool's Talk: Recovering the Art of Christian Persuasion* (Downers Grove, IL: InterVarsity Press, 2015), 32.

3. J. R. R. Tolkien, *Monsters and the Critics: And Other Essays* (UK: HarperCollins, 1997).

4. Paul Tripp, *A Quest for More: Living for Something Bigger* (Greensboro, NC: New Growth Press, 2007), 145.

5. John Newton and William Cowper, *Olney Hymns in Three Books* (Glasgow: William Collins, 1829), 293.

6. Bob Kauflin, *Worship Matters: Leading Others to Encounter the Greatness of God* (Wheaton, IL: Crossway Books, 2008), 25.

7. C. S. Lewis, *Reflections on the Psalms* (London: Harvest/Harcourt, 1958), 95.

8. Amy Carmichael, "A Song of Lovely Things" in *Mountain Breezes: The Collected Poems of Amy Carmichael* (Fort Washington, PA: CLC Publications, 2013).

9. Carol Cymbala, "I'm Clean" ©1983 Word Music, LLC and Carol Joy Music.

10. Tim and Kathy Keller, *The Songs of Jesus* (New York: Penguin, 2015), viii.

11. Mark Ashton, R. Kent Hughes, Timothy J. Keller, ed. D. A. Carson, *Worship by the Book* (Grand Rapids, MI: Zondervan, 2002), 30.

12. Eugene H. Peterson, *As Kingfishers Catch Fire: A Conversation on the Ways of God Formed by the Words of God* (New York: WaterBrook, 2017), 60.

13. Henry David Thoreau, *Walden* (New York: Thomas Y. Crowell & Co., 1910), 8.

14. Joni Eareckson Tada, www.brainyquote.com/quotes/quotes/j/jonieareck526378.html?src=t_forces.

15. Mark Noll, "We Are What We Sing," *Christianity Today*, July 12, 1999, 37.

16. Sally Goddard Blythe, *The Genius of Natural Childhood: Secrets of Thriving Children* (Stroud, UK: Hawthorn Press, 2011).

17. Thomas A. Schafer, ed., *The Works of Jonathan Edwards, The "Miscellanies," a-500* (New Haven, CT: Yale University Press, 1994), Miscellanies 188.

18. David Kinnaman, *You Lost Me: Why Young Christians Are Leaving Church . . . and Rethinking Faith* (Grand Rapids, MI: Baker Books, 2011), 22.

19. Ibid., 28.

20. Ibid., 29.

21. Keith Getty and Stuart Townend, "The Power of the Cross," © 2005 Thankyou Music (PRS) (adm. worldwide at CapitolCMGPublishing.com excl. Europe which is adm. by Integritymusic.com).

22. Keith Getty and Stuart Townend, "O Church Arise (Arise, Shine)," © Copyright 2016 Getty Music Publishing (BMI) (Admin. by Music Services, www.musicservices.org/Thankyoumusic (PRS)/ Worship Together Music (BMI)/Sixsteps Songs (BMI)/S.D.G. Publishing (BMI) (Admin. at Capitalcmgpublishing.com.

23. Kenneth W. Osbeck, *101 Hymn Stories* (Grand Rapids, MI: Kregel Publications, 1982), 14.

24. Rico Tice, *Honest Evangelism* (England, UK: The Good Book Company, 2015), 83.

25. David Platt, *Radical* (Colorado Springs, CO: Multnomah, 2010), 7.

26. Fenggang Yang, "When Will China Become the World's Largest Christian Country?" *Slate*. Essay from "What Is the Future of Religion?" Accessed June 9, 2017, http://www.slate.com/bigideas/what-is-the-future-of-religion/essays-and-opinions/fenggang-yang-opinion.

27. Platt, *Radical*.

28. Keith Getty, Kristyn Getty, and Stuart Townend, "Come, People of the Risen King," Copyright (c) 2001 Thankyou Music (PRS) (adm. worldwide at CapitolCMGPublishing.com excl. Europe which is adm. by Integritymusic.com).

29. Bob Kauflin, *Worship Matters* (Wheaton, IL: Crossway Books, 2008), 37.